OUTLAWS & LAWMEN of Western Canada

Volume One

The original monument near the coulee in the Cyress Hills where in 1879 Constable M. Graburn was the first member of the RNWMP to be murdered. (See page 112.)

Copyright © 1986, 1999 Heritage House Publishing Company Ltd.

Canadian Cataloguing in Publication Data

Main entry under title:

Outlaws and lawmen of Western Canada

ISBN 1-895811-79-1 (v. 1)

1. Outlaws—Canada, Western—History. 2. Criminals—Canada,
Western—History. 3. Police—Canada, Western—History.
FC3217.1.A1O98 1999   364.1'092'2712   C99-910257-5
F1060.3.O98 1999

Printing History: First Edition - 1983
                   Reprinted - 1985, 1991, 1994
                   First Heritage House edition - 1999

Heritage House wishes to acknowledge Heritage Canada through the Book
Publishing Industry Development Program, the British Columbia Arts Council,
and the Canada Council for the Arts for supporting various aspects of our publishing
program.

Front cover: Painting by T.B. Pitman, courtesy RCMP.
Back cover: Two of the most important places in the western history of the NWMP are
Forts Whoop-Up and Macleod in what is now Alberta (see page 4). Both forts have been
rebuilt, Whoop-Up at Lethbridge and Macleod at Fort Macleod. The upper photo shows
the loop-holed bastion of Fort Whoop-Up and the house flag of the U.S. trading firm which
built the forts in the early 1870s as an outlet for its illegal whiskey. The flag has been
officially adopted by the City of Lethbridge. The lower photo shows Fort Macleod, its
mounted patrol, and one of the original cannon from Fort Whoop-Up. The restored forts
attract tens of thousands of visitors every year.

Photo credits: B.C. Provincial Archives 46, 50, 52, 78-79, 100, 101, 102-103, 106, 109;
Fort Macleod Museum back cover (bottom); Glenbow Archives 9, 35, 40, 42, 113, 116;
Heritage House 33, 124; Manitoba Archives 14-15, 56-57, 60, 64-65, 66, 68; Provincial
Archives of Alberta 70-71, 86-87, 90, 92-93, 116; Public Archives of Canada 16, 18, 20,
21, 23, 26-27, 34-35, 61; Royal Canadian Mounted Police 1, 7, 12, 24, 26-27, 29, 39, 86,
118-119; Saskatchewan Archives Board 96-97; Jean Brown 45, 54; Wiggs O'Neill 45;
John W. Sutherland 107.

HERITAGE HOUSE PUBLISHING COMPANY LTD.
Unit #8 – 17921 55th Ave., Surrey, B.C. V3S 6C4

Printed in Canada

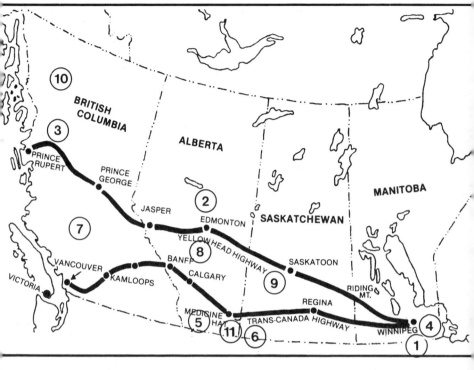

CONTENTS

Although their red tunics and white gauntlets were impressive, virtually none of the 275 men of the fledgling North-West Mounted Police were experienced. In addition, their rifles and revolvers were obsolete, their tents blew down in the wind, their pillbox hats were useless and their guides didn't know the way.

Nevertheless, in 1874 they left Manitoba on a 1,280-km (800-mile) overland trek to the lawless West. Despite dragging two unwieldy cannons and hardships that included water so scarce they drank diluted buffalo urine, they succeeded in what became the epic

March of the Mounties

THE LAWLESS LAND

In 1869 the fledgling Dominion of Canada agreed to give the Hudson's Bay Company some $1.5 million and land grants to relinquish its rights to Rupert's Land and its trading monopoly in what was then called The North-Western Territory. In return the Dominion gained control of a region from which evolved much of today's Quebec and Ontario, all of Manitoba, Saskatchewan and Alberta, and the Yukon and Northwest Territories. A Lieutenant-Governor and Council were appointed administrators and Prime Minister Sir John A. Macdonald decided to form a mounted police force to maintain order. Unfortunately, these plans were dropped and a region rivalling in size the United States became a land of no law.

Heretofore a semblance of order had been maintained by the Hudson's Bay Company that for some 200 years was the administrator of what law there was in the West. Under its jurisdiction, Chief Factors were given powers to try criminal cases and an endeavor was made to preserve

North-West Mounted Police escort the Duke of Cornwall and York at Calgary in 1901. The inset photo shows the Force's first Commissioner, G.A. French.

law and order for the benefit of profit and loss. Nevertheless, between 1778 when the white man first began to penetrate the plains on a regular and organized basis and 1874 when the North-West Mounted Police arrived, the question of crime and punishment was largely academic. Company posts were isolated, the white population small, and the Indian a law unto himself.

The Indian's philosophy of crime and punishment was uncomplicated. If a friend or relative was killed, you retaliated by slaying the slayer, or a member of his immediate family. Thus were the scales of justice balanced. The only problem was that retaliation frequently led to further retaliation, and avenger became victim. Nevertheless, a slaying seldom developed into a vendetta. By and large the Indian, acting in the heat of the moment, brought retribution for a killing and ended the bloodletting.

With the transfer from Hudson's Bay control a new element was introduced into the Indian way of life — unlimited liquor. Not that the HBC and other traders were teetotallers in their transactions with Indians. But they did exercise control on the sensible premise that drunken Indians made poor trappers and were unpredictable and very dangerous. In 1804 Alexander Henry, a trader for the North West Company at Pembina, noted in his journal: "Indians having asked for liquor and promised to decamp and hunt well all summer, I gave them some. Grand Gueule stabbed Capot Rouge, Le Boeuf stabbed his young wife in the arm, Little Shell almost beat his old mother's brains out with a club, and there was terrible fighting among them. I sowed garden seeds."

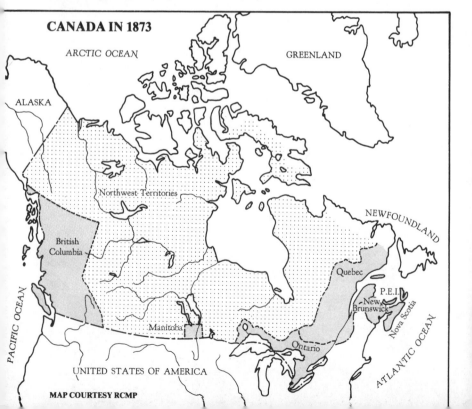

CANADA IN 1873

ARCTIC OCEAN

GREENLAND

ALASKA

Northwest Territories

NEWFOUNDLAND

British Columbia

Quebec

P.E.I.

New Brunswick

Nova Scotia

Manitoba

Ontario

PACIFIC OCEAN

ATLANTIC OCEAN

UNITED STATES OF AMERICA

MAP COURTESY RCMP

But not all traders peacefully sowed their seeds during the Indians' brawls. Some became the victims, their bodies lying in lonely graves. It was obvious to the businessmen of the Hudson's Bay Company that dead traders or dead Indians made them no profit. Hence they strove to have the Indians' way of life disturbed as little as possible, even to actively discouraging any settlement of their vast domain.

In the late 1860s, however, a dramatic change occurred in the form of aggressive Yankees from Montana Territory. The U.S. Civil War with its 600,000 dead soldiers was now history and covered wagons by the thousands rumbled across the plains carrying settlers to California, Oregon and other western regions. Among new communities to appear was Fort Benton on the Upper Missouri River about 160 km (100 miles) south of what would one day be Alberta.

Fort Benton became the supply area for a massive region of the U.S. plains and unprincipled "free traders" who ventured north to challenge the HBC trading monopoly. Their main stock-in-trade was whiskey. Without concern for its catastrophic consequences they dispensed it from trading posts, or forts as they called them, with colorful names such as Whiskey Gap, Robber's Roost, Fort Slide Out, Fort Stand Off, Spitzee Post and Fort Whoop-Up. The latter, near modern-day Lethbridge, became the focal point of the liquor traffic.

It was born in 1869 when John Jerome Healy and Alfred B. Hamilton, two U.S. traders from Fort Benton, built eleven log cabins at the junction of the St. Mary and Oldman Rivers. They surrounded the cabins

Blood Indians outside Fort Whoop-Up in 1874 before the arrival of the lawmen. Illegal whiskey was then rapidly destroying the Indians.

with a flimsy palisade and that winter netted $50,000. Unfortunately, the Indians set fire to it, feeling that they were being cheated — an assessment that was undoubtedly correct.

Hamilton and Healy, however, weren't about to leave so lucrative a land. They started another fort a few hundred feet away — one that wouldn't burn so easily. It was built of heavy, squared timbers with a sturdy palisade loopholed for rifles and two bastions complete with cannon. On one of the bastions was a flagpole from which fluttered Healy's personal flag — blue and red — which at a distance resembled the Stars and Stripes. The fort also had a bell like that on a locomotive which was rung when trading was to start.

The interior contained cookhouse, blacksmith shop, stables and living quarters with huge stone fireplaces. All windows were barred, as were the chimneys, since in their craving for whiskey Indians had broken into trading posts by dropping down the chimney. The post, called Fort Hamilton (but soon to be known as "Whoop-Up"), took thirty men two years to build and cost some $25,000.

Indians were seldom permitted inside the palisade. They pushed their buffalo hides and other items through a small wicket near the main gate and exchanged them for blankets, guns, and whiskey — particularly whiskey. When the furs were gone and the whiskey too, they traded not only the horses they needed to hunt the buffalo on which they survived, but their wives and even daughters as young as twelve.

"The firey (fiery) water flowed as freely as the streams running from the rocky Mountains," wrote a Catholic missionary, "and hundreds of poor Indians fell victims to the white man's craving for money, some poisoned, some frozen to death whilst in a state of intoxication, and many shot down by American bullets."

The (fiery) water referred to by the missionary was a brutal concoction. Each trader brewed his own, the motive to maximize profits. A typical recipe diluted one gallon of raw alcohol with three gallons of water. Then was added a pound of tea, a handful of red peppers, some Jamaica ginger, a pound of chewing tobacco and some Castille soap, Perry's Painkiller or even a dash of lye to give it "bite" since the Blackfoot liked whiskey that burned on the way down. The brew was brought to boil to blend the ingredients then ladled out in tin cups.

"I never knowed what made an Injun so crazy when he drank till I tried this booze . . . ." wrote cowboy author-artist Charles M. Russell. "You could even shoot a man through the brain or heart and he wouldn't die till he sobered up."

Probably the most damning indictment against the whiskey traders was written by the Reverend John McDougall, one of the West's renowned missionaries. He noted: "Scores of thousands of buffalo robes and hundreds of thousands of wolf and fox skins and most of the best horses the Indians had were taken south into Montana, and the chief article of barter for these was alcohol. In this traffic very many Indians were killed, and also quite a number of white men. Within a few miles of us . . . forty-two able-bodied men were the victims among themselves, all slain in the drunken rows. These were Blackfoot . . . . There was no law but might.

Some terrible scenes occurred when whole camps went on the spree, as was frequently the case, shooting, stabbing, killing, freezing, dying. "Thus these atrocious debauches were continuing all that winter not far from us. Mothers lost their children. These were either frozen to death or devoured by the myriad dogs of the camp. The birth-rate decreased and the poor red man was in a fair way towards extinction, just because some men, coming out of Christian countries, and themselves the evolution of Christian civilization, were now ruled by lust and greed."

In addition to missionaries, others including the United States Government, Hudson's Bay Company, and Canadian Pacific Railway urged the Dominion to form a mounted force to police the West. The Dominion Government responded in 1872 by sending Colonel Robertson-Ross, adjutant-general for the Canadian militia, to the West for an official opinion. On his return he promptly recommended that a mounted police force of 550 riflemen be established.

As a consequence, in May 1873 parliament passed a bill providing for the establishment of a "Police Force in the North-West Territories," and for magistrates, courts and jails. But a surprise obstacle was Prime Minister Sir John A. Macdonald. Not that he opposed the force. In fact he had been the primary motivation behind the legislation. But Macdonald was a marvelous procrastinator, so accomplished that he earned the nickname "Old Tomorrow." Now he put off implementing the legislation.

Fortunately, among those who recognized the desperate need for a Western police force was Alexander Morris. He had been a member of Macdonald's cabinet but resigned in 1872 to become lieutenant-governor of the province of Manitoba and the vast Northwest Territories. He continued to press for a police force, cautioning Macdonald that a "... most important matter ... is the preservation of order in the Northwest and little as Canada may like it she has to stable her elephant."

But even though the legislation to establish the police force had passed unanimously, Macdonald was in no hurry to "stable the elephant." In fact he didn't intend to begin recruiting until the next year.

A Crow Indian killed and scalped by the Bloods in 1874. With the arrival of white settlers in the West the incidence of scalping dramatically increased.

But though he didn't know it, there had already been a massacre of Indians in the West that was to change his leisurely schedule.

STABLING THE ELEPHANT

The Cypress Hills which straddle the southern border of what is today Alberta-Saskatchewan had for centuries been a favorite Indian region. Its miles of jackpine made excellent tipi poles and it was rich in buffalo, black and grizzly bear, deer and other wildlife.

The white men found it equally attractive, especially the whiskey traders. Among them were Abel Farwell and Moses Solomon who built whiskey forts nearly side by side deep in the Hills. In May 1873 a band of Assiniboine were camped near Farwell's post and, as later reported: "... whiskey flowed like water ... and by mid-day the tribesmen were all hopelessly drunk ...."

Probably nothing extraordinary would have happened but for the arrival of a party of wolfers — men who lived by poisoning wolves then

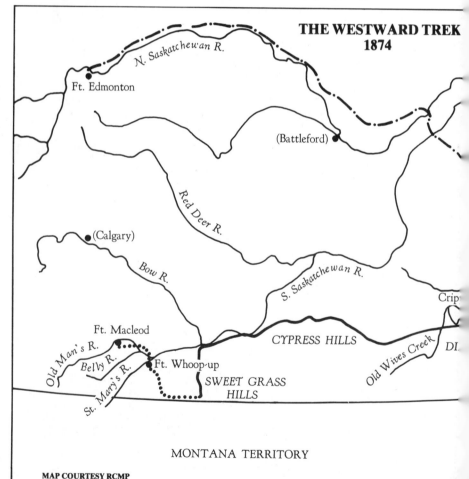

THE WESTWARD TREK
1874

N. Saskatchewan R.

Ft. Edmonton

(Battleford)

Red Deer R.

(Calgary)

Bow R.

S. Saskatchewan R.

Crip

Ft. Macleod

Old Man's R.

Belly R.

St. Mary's R.

Ft. Whoop-up

CYPRESS HILLS

Old Wives Creek

DI.

SWEET GRASS
HILLS

MONTANA TERRITORY

MAP COURTESY RCMP

● Ft. Benton

selling the hides. Wolfers were disliked by the Indians because their dogs were often among the poison victims. For their part these wolfers — later described as ". . . persons of the worst class in the country" — had no concern for either the dogs or the Indians they killed.

About noon on June 1 a man named Hammond who was staying at Farwell's post discovered that his horse was missing. He accused the Assiniboines and vowed to take two of theirs in retaliation. When he asked the wolfers to help, they eagerly grabbed their rifles and six- guns.

Who fired the first shot is uncertain, as is the number of Assiniboine men, women and children killed. Best estimates are that the wolfers massacred at least twenty Indians, including Chief Little Soldier. He was roused from a drunken stupor by his wife who attempted to lead him to the safety of the woods. He refused to go, and as he stood defenceless was murdered by one of the wolfers. Another Indian, an old man, was killed with a hatchet, his head severed then mounted on a lodge pole. Four women were taken to Solomon's post, among them Little Chief's wife.

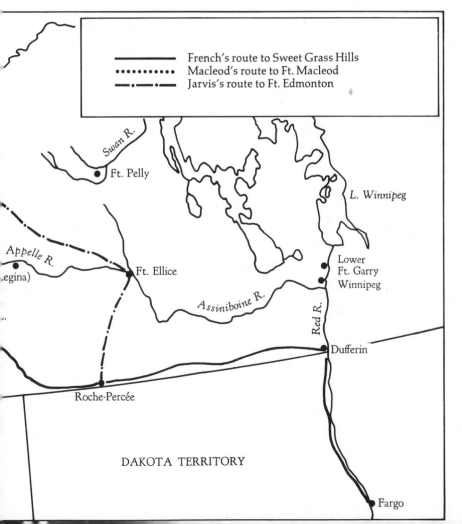

Here she and another young woman were repeatedly raped. Next morning the wolfers buried their only casualty, Ed Legrace, under the floor of Farwell's post, burned it and Solomon's, then hurriedly left.

News of the slaughter was three months reaching Ottawa and even then came via U.S. authorities. While there was indignation over the fact that "... defenceless Canadian Indian women and children had been murdered by the U.S. renegades . . . " Macdonald still held back his recruiting schedule. Then on September 20 he received a telegram from the needling Lieutenant-Governor Morris: "What have you done as to Police Force? Their absence may lead to grave disaster."

This time the Prime Minister acted. On September 25, 1873, the first officers were appointed and recruiting began for 150 men. The lowest rank, sub-constable, was to receive 75 cents a day, rations and clothing, and a free grant of 160 acres in the Northwest Territories on the satisfactory completion of his three-year enlistment.

In early October the new recruits — only two of whom had been

The earliest known photo of the force, taken in 1874. Seated is Sub-Inspector John French, brother of Commissioner G. A. French, later killed during the Riel Rebellion. Standing behind French is Sub-Inspector F. J. Dickens, son of author Charles Dickens.

policemen — left Ontario for Lower Fort Garry, about 32 km (20 miles) north of today's Winnipeg. They travelled in comfort by lake steamer to the head of Lake Superior, then challenged some 720 km (450 miles) of a route established by the fur traders. It consisted mostly of rivers and lakes and included dozens of portages, some up to two miles long. The recruits passed their first test well. When they arrived at the fur trading post the *Winnipeg Manitoban* reported: "Judging from the first detachment, the Mounted Police are a fine body of men."

But when the force's temporary commander, Lieutenant-Colonel W. Osborne Smith, swore in the men he must have wondered about the potential effectiveness of the "fine body of men." Most were without uniforms, arms and other gear because everything had been frozen in between Fort Garry and Lake Superior. Worse, most of the horses were unbroken, with few of the recruits able to ride anything more vigorous than a rocking chair.

Despite these problems, training started immediately. The routine was brutal. From reveille at 6 a.m. — changed to 6.30 during the coldest winter months — until long after dark the recruits participated in foot drill, marksmanship, riding, stable cleaning and other duties. In charge of breaking the horses and teaching recruits to ride was Sergeant-Major Samuel B. Steele, destined to become the most famous of all the Mounties. He later wrote: ". . . the orders were that if the temperatures were not lower than 36 below zero the riding and breaking should go on.

"With very few exceptions the horses were bronchos which had never been handled and . . . even when we had them 'gentled' so as to let the recruits mount, the men were repeatedly thrown with great violence to the frozen ground; but no-one lost his nerve . . . ."

In his training Steele was impartial. One day a semi-broken horse threw its rider heavily, kicking him for good measure in the back of his breeches. After watching the performance, Steele called for someone to catch "that poor horse." Then, after a pause, added: "And while you're at it, carry that awkward lout off the parade square." The fact that the "lout" was his brother, Dick, didn't impress Sam. "With plenty of such exercise," he recalled, "when spring opened they were very fine riders . . . ."

On June 19 the men were sent south to Dufferin near the Manitoba-Dakota Territory border. Here they were joined by another 217 officers and men who had been recruited during the winter and trained at Toronto. Among the new contingent was Joseph Francis, a Crimean War veteran who had taken part in the famous Charge of the Light Brigade. Another was trumpeter Fred A. Bagley, at fifteen the youngest of the policemen.

By now the force had an offical uniform which included a scarlet Norfolk jacket, steel grey breeches, blue trousers with a double white stripe and a dark blue cloak. Footwear was long black or brown boots with spurs, headgear a pill-box hat or a white helmet with matching white gauntlets.

But while uniforms were impressive, the force's most important equipment, their firearms, were not. Rifles were Snider-Enfield single shot, already obsolete. Indians and whiskey traders were using the much superior repeating rifles such as Winchester or Henry. Not for four years would the policemen be issued with Winchesters.

Their revolvers were also inferior. With many of them the chambers wouldn't revolve when the trigger was pulled but had to be turned with both hands. The six-guns in use in the West didn't have this defect.

Another problem was the lack of information about the West. There were not over 100 settlers in the entire region, most of them at Portage la Prairie 80 km (50 miles) west of Fort Garry. The only map was one made by the Palliser Expedition during an exploratory trip for the British Government in 1857-61. While it accurately showed the expedition's route, most of the map was based on information received from traders and half-breeds and proved remarkably unreliable. The policemen's primary objective, Fort Whoop-Up, was found to be some 130 km (80 miles) from its supposed location.

The degree of opposition was another unknown. A newspaper reported that 500 outlaws in forts and armed with repeating rifles awaited the men. Even Commissioner French expected "hot work" once they found the whiskey traders. Then there were the Indians, particularly the warlike Blackfoot Nation who resented the white intrusion. Against their reported 2,000 warriors the only support the *Toronto Mail* newspaper could give to the policemen was the hope that if they were scalped then:
"Sharp be the blade and sure the blow,
and short the pang to undergo."
Small wonder that fifteen-year-old Fred Bagley's mother urged him

to ". . . say your prayers regularly . . . ." Youthful Bagley was to serve for twenty-five years, although he little realized that in forthcoming days his lips would be so swollen from the sun, dust and thirst that he would be unable to sound bugle calls.

The force left Dufferin on July 8 with a "Hudson's Bay" start — they travelled a short distance then camped for the night to ensure that nothing was forgotten. The next morning two wagon loads of surplus supplies and gear were sent back to Dufferin and replaced with oats.

MARCH OF THE MOUNTIES

The following day under its thirty-two-year-old leader, Commissioner George A. French, the force began to march west. Its primary mission, as outlined by Governor-General Lord Dufferin, was ". . . capturing a band of desperadoes who had established themselves in some fortified posts in our territory in the neighbourhood of the Belly River." Other duties included gaining the respect and confidence of the Indians and aiding settlement.

To accomplish this gigantic task — one that across the border involved thousands of U.S. soldiers — were 275 officers and men. Several had to be left behind because of typhoid and other sickness and two died, the force's first casualties. In addition to the men there were 310 horses,

Boundary Commission wagons near Long River in 1872. Commissioner French wanted to follow their rough trail along the border. The politicians, however, decreed that he had to traverse the trackless prairie through a region that offered little forage, wood or water.

"A Lancer of the N.W.M.P." by artist-journalist Henri Julien who accompanied the force on its westward trek. There are no known photos of the march, and Julien's sketches are the only visual record.

142 oxen, 93 head of cattle, 114 Red River carts, 73 wagons, two 9-pounder field guns, and two mortars. Mowers, ploughs and similar farming implements accompanied the men. Wherever they established a post they would not only have to build it but grow their own grain and vegetables. When closed up the cavalcade stretched for 2.5 km (1½ miles) but more frequently was strung out over double that distance.

On the westward trek Commissioner French wanted to follow a trail built by the Boundary Commission during their 1872-74 survey of the U.S.-Canada border. This route would give him accurate information about the location of feed and water. But the politicians ordered otherwise. He was to follow the border some 320 km (200 miles) only, head north, then westward. This decision, made by people who had never seen the West, forced the men to weeks of travel through a parched plain where waterholes were infrequent and the livestock had to compete for grass with buffalo, grasshoppers and prairie fires. As a consequence, scores of horses and oxen died and the men were condemned to days of unnecessary suffering.

Four days after they left Dufferin, French wrote an entry in his diary he would constantly repeat: "Camped beside a marshy pool which had dried up. Got a few buckets of water by digging in mud . . . no wood or water."

To avoid the heat of the noon sun, reveille was often at 3 a.m. The cavalcade was underway an hour later, with 6 a.m. considered a late start. But the lack of feed, the heat, and the clouds of mosquitoes quickly incapacitated many horses. Ten days on the way French noted: ". . . two horses left on road, being unfit to travel."

Next day two more were left and the following day two died. On July 22 French wrote: "No wood or water during morning march or afternoon march . . . . I insisted on men dismounting and walking on foot every alternate hour and propose continuing this to relieve the horses."

In addition to men and animals struggling all day in the heat without water they were harassed by mosquitoes. Among those on the trip was Henri Julien, staff artist for *The Canadian Illustrated News*. Although he was an experienced outdoorsman from Eastern Canada, well familiar with mosquitoes, he wrote: ". . . all agreed that nowhere had they seen anything to equal the mosquito of the prairie.

". . . As soon as twilight deepens, they make their appearance on the horizon, in the shape of a cloud, which goes on increasing in density as it approaches to the encounter. At first, a faint hum is heard in the distance, then it swells into a roar as it comes nearer. The attack is simply dreadful . . . ."

"If you open your mouth to curse at them, they troop into it. They insinuate themselves under your clothes, down your shirt collar, up your sleeve cuffs, between the buttons of your shirt bosom. And not one or a dozen, but millions of them.

"You can brush them off your coat sleeves in layers. In the Mississippi valley, mosquitoes are warded off by a gauze net. In our (Eastern) Canadian backwoods the smoke of a big fire drives them away. But up here, they would tear a net to shreds, and put out a fire by the mere superincumbent weight of their numbers . . . . They sent a dog off howling in pain. They tease horses to desperation."

On July 25 because of the steady weakening of the animals, Commissioner French changed his plans. His original orders were for the entire force to keep together to the foothills of the Rockies. Then they would split into three groups — one remaining, one going northward to Fort Edmonton, the third returning to Fort Ellice. But so far they had travelled fewer than 480 km (300 miles) of the easiest part of their estimated 1,290 km (800 miles) and it was obvious that many — if not most — of the animals would die. French countermanded orders by sending "A" Division northward to Fort Ellice where a fur-traders' cart trail led to Fort Edmonton.

Inspector W.D. Jarvis left on July 29 with Sergeant-Major Sam Steele on the 1,450-km (900-mile) trek to Fort Edmonton. With them went 24 wagons, 55 carts, 20 men, and the weakest of the livestock. They reached Fort Edmonton on October 27 after a dreadful journey which included

"Storm on the Third of August" Julien called the above sketch. Virtually all of the force's tents blew down during the night. Julien felt that the half-breeds' tent was far superior to the military type which he called ". . . a fraud on the prairie . . . ."

continuing problems with the weak animals and, in contrast with the main body, too much water.

"Our loose horses very often fell," Steele later wrote, "one fine animal being lifted bodily by (Corporal) Carr and myself at least a dozen times by means of a pole. The other horses had to be helped along in the same manner until we arrived . . . .

". . . The trail was worse than any we had encountered. It was knee-deep in black mud, sloughs crossed it every hundred yards, and the wagons had to be unloaded and dragged through them by hand."

Of the horses, Inspector Jarvis was later to summarize: "They were living skeletons."

While Jarvis and his group were battling toward Fort Edmonton, Commissioner French and the remainder of the main force trudged westward. They reached the Boundary Commission's post at Wood Depot the same day that Jarvis left. Here they remained all day ". . . to allow men to cook and bake 3 days rations, and secure a supply of wood for 3 more days, as it is doubtful whether we will be able to get wood for a week . . . ."

Some of the policemen evidently did not take too seriously the necessity of carrying wood. Four days later French observed: ". . . no wood. Those Troops that did not carry enough wood on their waggons are now beginning to feel the effects of their thoughtlessness . . . ."

On August 4 a fierce storm now created additional discomfort. "My tent was blown completely away," artist Julien wrote, "and so were many others in camp . . . . These military tents are a fraud on the prairie, as we had more than one occasion to experience. As usual, the half-breeds managed such things better. There is nothing better than their low-roofed tent . . . . It is the warmest, easiest to set up, and the most comfortable."

The same night a new hazard identified itself. "Two men lost last night," French wrote, "had a gun and rocket fired: they both, fortunately, turned up all right to-day, being pretty well frightened at the idea of being so easily lost on the prairie . . . ."

The seeming endlessness of the prairie impressed not only the two men who were lost. "The prairies over which we travelled presented the same undulating, monotonous appearance," Julien wrote. "Not one green bush of the most dwarfish size to relieve the eye . . . . The eye dwells on vacancy, tired of glancing at the blue sky above or the brown earth beneath. A feeling of weariness creeps over you, interrupted at intervals by vague longings for something beyond the far low line of the horizon, which is ever barred across your vision. The silence is oppressing . . . . This has truly been called 'The Great Lone Land'.

"To add to our discomforts on this day's march, old Welsh, the guide, lost his bearings and led us miles out of the way . . . ."

French by now realized that his guides were unreliable and kept a check on directions and distance with a prismatic compass and an odometer. "Had a long pow-wow with guides," noted one diary entry. "Found that one of them was a regular imposter . . . ."

On April 12 they received their first visit from the Sioux Indians. French wrote: "It appears there has been a fight near the Cypress Hills

. . . . The half-breed and Sioux appear to have killed all the Black-feet . . . ."

Next day there was a formal meeting where French was given the name "Wachasta Sota," or "Man with Power." The Indians entertained the policemen with "dance and song" and the singer ". . . being one of the party in the late fight, and having scalped a Blackfoot, he felt pretty good over it . . . ."

On the 19th French decided to leave the sickest men and weakest animals until they returned on the homeward journey. At this aptly named "Cripple Camp" he left Constable Sutherland and 7 men, 12 wagons and 26 sick and weak horses.

On September 2 they saw their first buffalo and killed five. From one they got 953 pounds of meat; from the other, 767 pounds. But as French noted: ". . . there is nothing to show for the three others which had been killed, the half breeds merely cutting slices of the meat off . . . ."

The September 3 entry contains a familiar observation: "There being

Artist Henri Julien titled the above and opposite on-the-scene sketches "Dead Horse Valley" and "The Sweet Grass Hills in Sight." By then the horses and oxen were dying so rapidly and the men so exhausted that Commissioner French became alarmed for the safety of the force.

no grass had to make a sketch (stretch) of 17½ miles without halting. Next stage 20 miles, no water.''

DILUTED BUFFALO URINE TO DRINK

Of this phase of the journey Sub-Constable E.H. Maunsell wrote: "Although it was fortunate that we had buffalo meat to eat, being out of provisions, still straight boiled meat soon palled on the palate. We were all attacked with diarrhea, which greatly weakened us. Not only did we eat boiled buffalo meat, using their dried dung for fuel, but on occasions were forced to drink diluted buffalo urine.

"It was now September," he explained. "Many of the lakes we stopped at were just puddles. Thousands of buffalo had watered here all summer, and the only liquid we found was what was left in the tracks made by the buffalo. This we would dip out with a cup and boil, (adding lots of tea) but it was a most nauseating drink. Still, when one is without water for perhaps 24 hours he will drink anything. Our poor horses

suffered greatly, both from lack of food and water . . . ."

Adding to their problems were the cannon. As Julien noted: "Our two pieces of artillery were the most difficult of all to manage, weighing 4,400 lbs . . . . They were always in the way, retarded our march, took up the time of several men and the service of several good horses. They were not fired off even once at an enemy, and, in fact, had hostilities been encountered, would have been of less use than the rifles which the gunners should have carried."

On September 6 French had more problems when his guide insisted that they had reached the Bow River, their preliminary destination. "I told him we were at least 70 miles from the Bow," French wrote. "We have in fact reached the South Saskatchewan . . . . The Scout has brought us nearly a day's march out of our road during the last two days . . . . I am not quite sure whether his actions are due to ignorance or design. He is the greatest liar I have ever met. He is suspected as being a spy for the (Fort) Whoop up villians, but there is nothing definite or tangible to show this . . . ."

On September 8 the weather changed to cold rain with heavy wind. The next day five horses died, "paralyzed with cold and hunger," and the following day two more. To protect the animals French had each officer and man donate one of their blankets to cover the horses. In addition, everyone was now walking much of the time to spare the horses.

"I began to feel very much alarmed for the safety of the Force," French wrote. "If a few hours' cold rain kills off a number of horses, what would be the effect of a 24 hours snow storm . . . ?"

Fortunately, the weather held, unlike the year before when a three-day September blizzard swept the area, killing animals and men. On September 12 they reached the junction of the Belly and Bow Rivers, the supposed location of the whiskey traders' Fort Whoop-Up. There was neither fort not traders ready for battle.

Instead, French wrote: "The Fort!!! at the Forks of the Bow and Belly Rivers turns out to be three log huts without roofs in which some fellows occasionally stopped when trapping or rather poisoning wolves . . . ." French would have been even more upset had he known that the fort was some 130 km (80 miles) away and that the policemen would be another month reaching it.

While not finding the fort was a disappointment for French, another aspect of the false information was nearly disastrous. He had been assured that the region was one with luxurious pasture, "a perfect garden of Eden."

Instead he found that ". . . .at least sixty or seventy miles in every direction is little better than a desert, not a tree to be seen anywhere, ground parched and poor, and wherever there was a little swamp it was destroyed by the buffalo."

French had hoped to remain in the area a week to give his dying animals a chance to recover. But ". . . the Force had to leave there as quickly as possible to prevent their being actually starved to death . . . ."

On September 13-14 another nine horses died from cold and hunger. French decided to head south to a region called the Sweet Grass Hills where, the guides assured him, grass and water were plentiful. This time they were correct and on the 18th the force camped in a coulee not far from the Montana border. The day before three horses had dropped on the road, another in camp, while all the oxen had to be abandoned since they were too weak to travel. The men were little better, being exhausted by the long hours of pushing wagons, and suffering poor water and food that consisted mostly of buffalo, flour and dried potatoes. Their once red tunics were dirty and torn and many whose boots had worn out wore sacks on their feet.

After resting a few days, French, Assistant Commissioner J.F. Macleod and eight others left for Fort Benton on the Upper Missouri River some 160 km (100 miles) to the south. Free of the wagons and cumbersome cannon they made fast progress. "Made about 42 miles," French noted on the first day. On the third day, after crossing the Maria and Teton Rivers eleven times, they rode into Benton at noon.

Blood Indians outside the stout walls of Fort Whoop-Up in 1881.

At Fort Benton French purchased moccasins, boots, gloves, stockings for his men, corn and oats for the horses. He was surprised to find that the merchants, many of whom were deeply involved in the whiskey trade and should have resented the arrival of the police, were friendly. Isaac Baker, who had financed construction of Fort Whoop-Up for his nephew, Alfred B. Hamilton, was especially co-operative. He not only told French the location of the elusive fort but described the good wagon trail leading to it from Benton. He also introduced him to Jerry Potts, a half-breed guide.

French hired Potts for $90 a month, a move with immense benefit to the force. Heretofore they had more or less wandered westward across the plains. Now they had a guide who proved a plainsman without parallel and would loyally serve until his death twenty-two years later. Sam Steele would summarize Jerry's guiding ability in these words: "As scout and guide I have never met his equal, he had none in either the North West or the States to the south."

Potts was also an outstanding warrior whose early life illustrated the consequences of unlimited liquor mixed with a land of no law. He was the

A group of NWMP in the late 1870s. The officer with his hand on the horse is Commissioner J. F. Macleod.

son of Andrew Potts, a Scot employed by the American Fur Company, and a Blood Indian. While Potts was still a baby his father was murdered by a Peigan Indian. For the next few years he was cared for by Alexander Harvey, a man whose contempt for Indians was typical of most plainsmen. In the early 1840s, because his negro employee had been murdered, he fired a cannon into a group of unsuspecting Blackfoot Indians, killing thirteen. Whether or not the Blackfoot were guilty was of no interest to Harvey. Thirteen Indians, innocent or guilty, was the only just revenge, as far as he was concerned.

Fortunately for Potts, irate citizens forcefully urged Harvey to settle elsewhere. Potts was then cared for by Andrew Dawson. He not only taught Jerry English and five Indian dialects, but instilled in him an understanding and pride for both his white and Indian heritage. Jerry also became a superb horseman and a superb shot with six-gun or rifle.

In 1872 when Potts was in his early thirties he learned that his half-brother had been murdered by a drunken Blood Indian named Good Young Man and his mother killed when she tried to retrieve her son's body. Jerry vowed revenge. About two months later Good Young Man left camp to go hunting and Jerry shot him.

Potts participated in many of the Indian battles that characterized the region until the police arrived, including the last major Indian battle on Canadian soil. Involved were the Blackfoot and the Bloods, and the Crees and Assiniboines. The Crees started the fight by murdering several Blood squaws and a brother of Red Crow, the Blood chief. Unfortunately for the Crees, the Bloods and their allies were more plentiful and better armed. Once they recovered they routed the attackers. The battle was fought near today's Lethbridge and as the Crees attempted to escape by crossing the Oldman River they were picked off by the score. Potts, who had been elected leader and led a final charge that routed the Crees, later recalled: "You could fire with your eyes shut and still kill a Cree."

As John Peter Turner noted in his book, *The North-West Mounted Police*, the official history of the force: "Potts returned from the bloody affray with 19 grisly scalps, a deep head wound, and an arrow in his body. He had won imperishable fame."

As his first assignment for the Mounties, Potts guided French back to the Sweet Grass Hills. In compliance with his orders, French handed command over to Macleod and left to rejoin "D" and "E" Troops who had already begun the 1,290-km (800-mile) trek to a new headquarters near Fort Pelly. Macleod and the rest of the force turned northward toward Fort Whoop-Up.

On the way they learned that in addition to being a superb plainsman, their new guide was sparing with words. After four days of marching and riding and feeling that the elusive fort must be close, one of the officers asked Jerry: "What do you think is beyond that next hill, Jerry?"

"Nudder damn hill," was the reply.

The bullet-ridden body of an Indian along the trail provided another example not only of Jerry's brevity but also of the havoc caused by the whiskey traders. In answer to a query about the probable cause of the Indian's death, Jerry answered with one word: "Drunk." (For more information on Jerry Potts see Frontier Booklet No. 14, *Canadian Plainsmen: Gabriel Dumont — Jerry Potts.*)

FORT WHOOP-UP AND THE WHISKEY TRADERS

When the force finally reached Fort Whoop-Up on October 9 Macleod anticipated a fight, despite Jerry's assessment that the whiskey peddlers had fled. Macleod deployed his cannon and with his men rode toward the fort, the only movement the trader's flag fluttering above the bastion. With Potts at his side Macleod rode straight ahead, his men every second expecting rifles to blast from the loopholed palisade. Then Macleod halted, dismounted and strode through the wide open gate. He entered the silent fort and knocked on the door of the nearest building. A bearded, grey-haired trader named Dave Akers opened it and invited the police "to come right in." He was the only white occupant. As Potts had predicted, the whiskey traders left with their whiskey when they learned about the approaching police.

Akers had his Indian woman — one old-timer credited him with purchasing forty during his years on the plains — prepare a meal of buffalo meat and vegetables grown at the fort. Macleod offered to buy Whoop-Up as headquarters for $10,000, but Akers wanted $25,000. Since Macleod didn't have this much money he decided to build his own post. Jerry led them some 100 km (60 miles) to the northwest to an island in the Oldman River. Here was plenty of grass, water, and timber to build a fort. Work started immediately on the first NWMP post in the West, named Fort Macleod on orders from Commissioner French.

The storied Fort Whoop-Up didn't have long to survive. Akers continued trading — but not whiskey — and raising prize-winning cabbages in the compound. In 1888 fire destroyed much of the Fort, then in 1894 Akers was shot dead by his former partner, Tom Purcell.

Unfortunately for Purcell, the lawless era was history. He was promptly arrested by the Mounties but on pleading self-defence was given a jail sentence instead of being hanged.

A sketch of Fort Macleod drawn in 1874 by R. B. Nevitt, Assistant Surgeon during the force's westward trek.

Fort Whoop-Up in 1881. The men are standing near the main gate and the corner bastion which once held a cannon.

But Purcell was only one of scores who experienced the consequences of the new era of law and order. Even while the policemen were living in tents and rushing to complete Fort Macleod before the onset of blizzards and sub-zero temperatures, patrols searched for whiskey traders. On October 30, only a few days after they arrived, Colonel Macleod noted in a report to Commissioner French that we have "struck a first blow at the liquor traffic in this country."

Macleod had learned from an Indian named Three Bulls that a negro, William Bond, had a whiskey post at Pine Coulee some 80 km (50 miles) from Fort Macleod. Here Bond had traded Three Bulls two gallons of whiskey for two horses. It was a satisfactory transaction for Bond since horses were worth some $200 each, the whiskey perhaps one-twentieth that amount. Three Bulls felt he had been short-changed and decided to test the fairness of the red-coated horsemen that everyone was talking about.

As a result, a patrol under Inspector L.N. Crozier arrested Bond and four others. The policemen confiscated two wagons containing cases of alcohol, 16 horses, 5 Henry rifles, 5 revolvers, and 116 buffalo robes which became warm clothing for the ill-clad policemen. All those involved were fined, a sentence which led to identifying a leading figure in the whiskey trade. He was J.B. Weatherwax, a prominent Montana business-man with contempt for anything resembling law and order. He paid the fines of all except Bond, who was kept at the police post to serve his sentence. As yet the policemen were too busy building shelters for their animals and themselves — the stables were built before the barracks — to spend time on a jail.

As a result, on December 2 Bond escaped while being taken from one building to another. As he sprinted away, one of the guards fired but there was no obvious result. Under the harsh discipline of the force, those responsible for guarding Bond were sentenced to jail, although the whiskey trader paid heavily for being the first man to escape custody.

Next spring his body was found a few miles from the fort, a bullet between his shoulders. By now Colonel Macleod had learned that Bond was wanted for murder in Ontario and had also deliberately killed a Black-foot Indian. Who killed Bond is unknown, although the bullet fired by the guard was probably the cause.

As a result of arresting Bond and the other traders, the police learned the location of two more whiskey forts. Despite blizzards and below zero weather, in February nine men under Inspector Crozier with Jerry Potts as guide left Fort Macleod to arrest the traders. Their destination was about 160 km (100 miles) to the northwest but because of blizzards and cold they were eighteen days on the trek. On one occasion several of the policemen lost the trail during a storm but were found by Potts, even though visibility was less than 30 m (100 ft.). Of the incident Sergeant W.D. Antrobus noted in his diary: "This Jerry Potts is justly called the best guide in the country for I do not believe there is another man who could have guided us through the storm as he did."

Among those arrested during the frigid trek were several of Weatherwax's men. Weatherwax himself was rounded up by another mid-winter patrol of five policemen. It was led by Sub-Inspector Cecil E.

Denny who later wrote: "The weather was bitterly cold, and the snow deep. A pack-horse carried our bedding, a small tent, and a few provisions."

Denny and two policemen surprised Weatherwax and two other men drinking and playing cards in a big log house. "Had they not been taken by surprise," he wrote, "they would no doubt have offered resistance." The policemen found a large stock of liquor and hundreds of furs and robes. The men were arrested and taken to Fort Macleod on a trip that took three days. Here they were fined $250 by Macleod, with their teams, robes and other possessions confiscated.

Weatherwax, a tall imposing man, was, Denny noted: ". . . most defiant, threatening dire consequences to follow an appeal he should make to Washington. He failed to impress Colonel Macleod, who told him to pay his fine or go to jail, and so far as an appeal to Washington was concerned he was welcome to go the limit. He spent a week in the guard-room; then as hard labour was the lot of all prisoners — wood-cutting, stable-cleaning, and other jobs — he paid his fine and was released . . . ."

When news of Weatherwax's arrest and sentence reached Fort Benton the local newspaper indignantly noted: "Wherever the British flag floats, might is right, but we had no idea that the persons and property of American citizens would be trifled with in the manner that American merchants have been." The paper suggested that American troops march north so that ". . . the Bull-dogs would be properly chained and controlled."

A NWMP patrol with lances at Fort Walsh in 1878.

Since the newspaper was owned by J.B. Healy, one of the men who had skinned the Indians at Fort Whoop-Up, the criticism was understandable. But Healy and Weatherwax had already learned something that would be proved over and over — the Mounted Police didn't scare worth a cent. Some of them, however, died while helping to build this reputation.

The first member to die in the West was Constable Godfrey Parks. On October 26 he died of typhoid and became the first occupant of a cemetery established between Fort Macleod and the river. Just over two months later he was joined by two others. On December 30 Constables Baxter and Wilson left Fort Macleod for Fort Kipp but were caught in a sudden storm. When their riderless horses reached Fort Kipp a search was started by Blackfoot trackers. They soon found Baxter's lifeless body, then Wilson. He was alive but died shortly afterward.

Despite these tragedies the force continued its pressure on the whiskey peddlers. By the spring of 1875 the trade had declined abruptly from a flourishing enterprise to a minor nuisance. Without a shot the policemen had swiftly accomplished their primary mission — and built their outpost of Fort Macleod at the same time. One of the first men arrested, Harry "Kamoose" Taylor, settled at Fort Macleod and became a prominent hotel owner. Even Weatherwax mellowed. He became a wealthy Montana

Protecting the thousands of settlers who populated the prairies from the 1880s was one duty of the NWMP. Every inhabitant was listed and checked regularly. In one year alone horse patrols from Regina travelled nearly 600,000 km (350,000 miles) visiting farms like the one below near Lloydminster in the early 1900s.

rancher and a staunch admirer of the red-coated "Riders of the Plains."

The lawmen were equally successful in their second objective — winning the friendship of the Indians. When the Blackfoot nation gathered in 1877 to sign the treaty confining them to reservations, Crowfoot, their legendary chief who had been wounded over a dozen times in his many battles, summarized his people's feelings: "If the Police had not come to the country, where would we all be now? Bad men and whiskey were killing us so fast that very few, indeed, of us would have been left to-day. The Police have protected us as the feathers of the bird protect it from the frosts of winter. I wish them all good, and trust that all our hearts will increase in goodness from this time forward. I am satisfied. I will sign the treaty."

In forthcoming years the mounted policemen completed the third of their initial objectives — overseeing the peaceful settlement by hundreds of thousands of people on 1,000 miles of Western plains. The biggest challenge to peace began in 1876 when the warlike Sioux retreated into Canada after slaughtering Lieutenant-Colonel George A. Custer and his entire 7th Cavalry. Eventually there were some 6,000 Sioux in the Cypress Hills under Chief Sitting Bull with only a few red coats under Superintendent J.M. Walsh to control them. Despite massive problems they succeeded and by 1881 all of the Indians had returned to the U.S.

During the Riel Rebellion the Mounties served with distinction, among them Sam Steele, who commanded a group of cowboys, settlers and policemen called "Steele's Scouts." Among those who died fighting

the rebels was John French, Commissioner George A. French's brother, who had resigned from the force in 1883 and was an officer in the militia. But so little did Ottawa bureaucrats and politicians appreciate the efforts of the policemen that while all citizen-soldiers received medals within one year, they had to wait three years. However, those men who had been scouts and were usually the first to be shot at weren't permitted medals. According to the politicians, safely out of range in the East, they hadn't "been in action," even though their companions had been wounded and killed. (Ironically, there would have been no uprising if Prime Minister Sir John A. Macdonald and the rest of the politicians had heeded the warnings of police and others and settled the just grievances of the Indians and Metis.)

The campaign ribbon wasn't the only example of shabby treatment. In 1879, the policemen's pay was virtually halved, with a sub-constable's reduced from 75 cents a day to 40 cents — and not returning to 75 cents for over a quarter century. As a further insult the free grant of 160 acres at the end of a satisfactory enlistment was cancelled. In 1883 at Fort Macleod the men staged a revolt to protest the conditions. For months they had been fed bread, beef and tea three times a day, the meat frequently fit only for garbage. Uniforms were not replaced and on their cut-rate wages the men had to borrow money and pay interest to feed and clothe themselves. Among clothing all men bought were Stetson cowboy hats since the pill-box type was useless for Western weather. The pill-boxes weren't officially replaced until about 1900, or twentyfive years after they were issued.

Young Fred Bagley, who made the force his career and retired a Sergeant-Major, recalled that they were issued butter for the first time in 1897 — and it was rancid. It had been sold to the government by a man who had a warehouse full, and arrived with instructions on how to prevent it from going even more rancid.

Yet despite the shabby treatment the men worked faithfully to uphold the motto of the force, "Maintain the Right." Among their duties in the 1890s, for instance, was protecting tens of thousands of prairie settlers, most of whom had never been out of the city. Hazards were fires which swept the plains with the speed of a galloping horse, blizzards which made venturing from house to barn perilous, injury, illness, and a host of other potentially disastrous situations. To help safeguard them, every inhabitant was listed and regular patrols started, each settler signing a patrol sheet when a Mountie checked. The area covered by horseback and by buggy was awesome. In one year out of Regina alone patrols travelled nearly 350,000 miles, a distance equivalent to four times around the world with a side trip to the moon.

Fred Bagley and his horse, Old Buck, knew these patrols well. Old Buck had made the march west with Bagley and the two remained together for years afterwards. Eventually the horse was pensioned but as Constable Gray Campbell wrote in the *RCMP Quarterly:* ". . . though he was effectively pensioned, no General Order to that effect managed to keep him from doing police work. His remaining years were spent patrolling his old district from Lethbridge to Pincher Creek. Despite the fact that his master could not make these trips with him, Old Buck (made the patrol alone, covering) the two days trip in fair time, habitually stopping off at Fort Macleod Barracks each patrol for water and feed . . . ."

By then L.W. Herchmer was the Force's fourth Commissioner and he worked hard to improve the deplorable conditions. One change that he effected was replacing the tents that artist Henri Julien had found so inadequate. One fault was that their shape didn't permit the use of bunks. As a consequence, the men slept on the ground, many getting rheumatism. Even in barracks the government refused to supply proper sleeping facilities. "The Indians at the Industrial School have beds!" Herchmer exclaimed in indignation. "Yet the police, the finest body of men in the country, still sleep on boards and trestles."

The first Commissioner, George A. French, had also fought for better conditions for his men. In 1874 he refused to make the new post at Swan River his headquarters as ordered since he felt that the barracks were unfit to live in. Because of a continuing clash with politicians he resigned in 1876. When he left his men collected money and presented him with a $200 gold watch and chain and his wife with a set of silver plate. He continued his career in the British Army, became a Major-General and was eventually knighted.

French summarized his feeling toward the men he commanded on the march and for their accomplishments in his December 1874 report: "A Canadian force, hastily raised, armed, and equipped, and not under martial law, in a few months marched 2,000 miles, through a country for the most part as unknown as it proved bare of pasture and scanty in the supply of water. Of such a march, under such circumstances, all true Canadians may well feel proud."

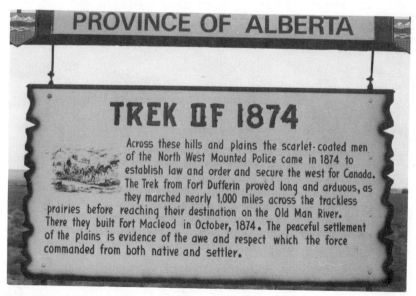

PROVINCE OF ALBERTA

TREK OF 1874

Across these hills and plains the scarlet-coated men of the North West Mounted Police came in 1874 to establish law and order and secure the west for Canada. The Trek from Fort Dufferin proved long and arduous, as they marched nearly 1,000 miles across the trackless prairies before reaching their destination on the Old Man River. There they built Fort Macleod in October, 1874. The peaceful settlement of the plains is evidence of the awe and respect which the force commanded from both native and settler.

The above Stop of Interest sign erected by the Alberta Government commemorates the March of the Mounties. It is located south of Milk River of Highway 4 which roughly follows the route of the 1869 Fort Benton — Fort Whoop-Up Trail.

Swift Runner—
The Cannibal

In the autumn of 1879 Swift Runner left on a trapping expedition with his brother, mother, wife and six children. During the winter he killed and ate them all, then complained that his mother was "a bit tough."

The problem of disposing of the victim's body has plagued murderers since the days of Cain. Burial, burning, dismemberment, acid and quicklime have been tried, but with no statistics it is impossible to recommend one method as superior to another. By and large, however, murderers tend to leave their victims where they fall, or at best make only a casual effort to conceal their crime. One exception was an Indian named

Swift Runner in jail and some of the evidence.

Swift Runner, notable primarily for the unique method he used to dispose of most of the evidence.

Swift Runner, or to give him his Indian name, Katist-chen, was a quiet, thoughtful man. For hours at a time he would sit immobile, a look of utter satisfaction on his face, staring into space. But beneath his calm exterior there lurked fires and tortures of a good old-fashioned Hell for at night Swift Runner was a troubled man. Again and again he would waken from his sleep, moaning that the Indian spirit of evil, Ween-de-go, was plaguing him with horrible dreams.

Swift Runner had appeared dramatically at the little Roman Catholic Mission at St. Albert, just north of Edmonton, in March 1879. To the kindly fathers, he unfolded a harrowing tale of despair and starvation. He had taken his wife, mother, brother and six children into the north woods around the Sturgeon River country, some eight miles from the Mission, for the winter hunt the previous fall. Never had the hunting been so bad, Swift Runner confided. In two months he found nothing to trap or shoot and by then their initial supply of food was exhausted. Growing weaker with hunger, his family had taken to their beds and attempted to lure friendly squirrels into their grasp. When the supply of squirrels and other small animals had been used up, as a last resort they cut their tent into strips, boiled it and chewed the pieces of rawhide for nourishment. The youngest child was the first to die. With their remaining strength they managed to dig a small grave in the forest. Swift Runner's mother and brother went off by themselves to find food and never returned. His wife, saddened as the other children died one by one, shot herself. Of the party of ten, only Swift Runner survived.

The Mission fathers were puzzled by some aspects of Swift Runner's story. For instance, other Indians returning from the woods brought news of good hunting. Nor did Swift Runner, who weighed nearly 200 pounds, have the appearance of a man who had survived such a terrible ordeal. Nevertheless, they appreciated that hunting could be good in one area, abominable in another, and the torture in the eyes of Swift Runner as he told his lamentable story was very real.

Swift Runner was given food and shelter and invited to stay at the Mission. Daily prayers were offered by the pious men for the tortured soul of the bereaved father, and the little Mission settled into its normal routine. As time passed, Swift Runner became a great favorite with the Indian children attending school at the Mission. He delighted them with tales of hunting in the north woods, or of bygone days when his people, the Crees, had warred with the ferocious Blackfoot nation to the south. But at night, Swift Runner's dreams were disturbed by the visitations of Ween-de-go. There were times when the priests, watching their strange guest playing with the children, were uneasy.

On the afternoon of May 25, 1879, the Indian boys came to Father Kemus, who was in charge of the Mission during Father Leduc's absence, seeking permission to accompany Swift Runner on a hunting expedition to the north. Faced with having to make a decision, Father Kemus could no longer suppress his doubts. It was true that Swift Runner had proved himself a gentle man, patient with children, reverent in his devotions and

Sub-Inspector Severe Gagnon | **Father Leduc**

obedient to the wishes of the priests, but the gnawing suspicion was not easily stilled. Withholding permission, Father Kemus went to the North-West Mounted Police barracks at Fort Saskatchewan and laid his problem before the skilled and experienced scrutiny of Sub-Inspector Severe Gagnon.

Gagnon had already received a circumspect message from the Indians around Egg Lake, Swift Runner's camping grounds, that the kindly Indian was one to be watched. Consequently, on hearing Father Kemus' fears, he immediately dispatched Sergeant Richard Steele and interpreter Brazeau, a trusted half-breed, to interview Swift Runner. But as they were unable to obtain a coherent report from Swift Runner, Sergeant Steele arrested him and brought him to Fort Saskatchewan on May 27.

Swift Runner's story was basically that his mother and brother had left, the children had died, one by one, and in the end his wife had killed herself. Sub-Inspector Gagnon was inclined to agree with his Sergeant's suspicions and on June 4, forcing the reluctant Swift Runner to accompany them, he left for the north with a party of police.

As they progressed towards the Sturgeon River country, the big Cree's good nature disappeared and he became sullen and stubborn. Twice he tried to escape from evening camps and twice he was recaptured. Where he had volunteered general information about the location of his winter camp, he now refused to answer all questions. It became evident that he was simply guiding them in a huge circle, and as he was the only one who knew the location of the camp, Gagnon began to despair of ever finding it. It was Brazeau, the interpreter, who solved the problem.

"We never get anywhere with that big Indian," Brazeau assured them. "Him too scared and too cunning. We give him 'the strong medicine'."

"No liquor," Gagnon warned.

The halfbreed interpreter only chuckled and went to prepare a batch of "strong medicine." He started by boiling a brew of tea and then, before the astonished eyes of the policemen, calmly added a large plug of chewing tobacco. The concoction he allowed to brew overnight.

The following morning Brazeau presented the evil smelling concotion to Swift Runner. He drank it with great gusto. Within a short while his good spirits resumed, then he began to talk and led the police to a clearing on a small, heavily wooded island in the middle of a lake. "This is where we camped," he informed them. "But as you can see, the bears have come and devoured the bodies."

With Swift Runner under close guard, Gagnon and his men began a thorough investigation of the camp. Strewn about the clearing and in the fringes of the trees they found the skulls of eight human beings. Around the campground were human bones, pieces of skin and knots of human hair.

Suddenly, Sergeant Steele was horrified by the discovery of a pair of baby's stockings stuffed into the eye socket of one of the skulls. They knew instantly that this was no depredation by prowling bears, but that they stood in the presence of a multiple murderer. As if to confirm their suspicions, they failed to find either bear tracks or claw marks. The tipi, supposed to have been eaten by the starving Indians, was located in the branches of a spruce tree some distance from the campsite. A few feet away, hidden in a clump of willow by the lake shore, they found a kettle, its insides thick with fat.

Certain now of the horrible truth, Sub-Inspector Gagnon ordered all the evidence carefully preserved and returned to Fort Saskatchewan to arraign Swift Runner for murder.

On August 16, 1879, Swift Runner was tried before Stipendiary Magistrate Richardson, assisted by two Justices of the Peace — E. McGillivray and George Verey. The jury of six comprised four men fluent in both English and Cree. On the witness stand Swift Runner changed his story, admitting that he had killed five of his six children as well as his wife. The sixth child had died of starvation. He stuck to his story that his mother and brother had left the party earlier.

After a trial that lasted two days, Swift Runner was found guilty. It took the jury only twenty minutes to decide that he had indeed killed his mother as well as his brother. Judge Richardson then sentenced him to be hanged on December 20, 1879.

In the guardroom while awaiting execution, Swift Runner was still troubled by the nightly visits of Ween-de-go. The kindly Father Kemus who visited him almost daily could do little to ease his soul. Towards the end of December, Father Leduc returned to Fort Saskatchewan and personally took over the ministrations to Swift Runner. Wise in the ways

The NWMP post of Fort Saskatchewan in the early 1880s.

St. Albert Mission in 1877. Here Swift Runner related his tale of despair and starvation, neglecting to mention that he had killed and eaten his entire family.

of his superstitious charges, Father Leduc warned him that he would never be free of his frightful nightmares until he told the truth about the hunting expedition.

Convinced, Swift Runner told a tale whose horror will seldom be matched in the annals of crime. Father Leduc translated it as follows:

"We were camped in the woods about eight miles from here," Swift Runner began. "In the beginning of winter we had not much to suffer. Game was plenty. I killed many moose and five or six bears; but about the middle of February I fell sick and to complete our misfortune those with me could find nothing to shoot. We had soon to kill our dogs and lived on their flesh while it lasted. Having recovered a little from my weakness, I travelled to a post in the Hudson's Bay Company on the Athabasca River and was assisted by the officer in charge, and returned to my camp with a small amount of provisions. That did not last us long. We all — that is, my mother, wife and six children (three boys and three girls) besides my brother and I — began to feel the pangs of hunger. My brother made up his mind to start with my mother in search of some game. I remained alone with my family. Starvation became worse and worse. For many days we had nothing to eat. I advised my wife to start with the children and follow on the snow and tracks of my mother and brother, who perhaps had been lucky enough to kill a moose or a bear since they left us. For my part, though weak, I hoped that remaining alone I could support my life with my gun. All my family left me with the exception of a little boy, ten years of age.

"I remained many days with my boy without finding any game and consequently without having a mouthful to eat. One morning I got up early and suddenly an abominable thought crossed my mind. My son was lying down close to the fire, fast asleep. Pushed by the evil spirits, I took my poor gun and shot him. The ball entered the top of his skull. Still he breathed. I began to cry, but what was the use. I then took my knife and sunk it twice into his side. Alas, he still breathed and I picked up a stick and killed him with it. I then satisfied my hunger by eating some of his flesh and lived on that for some days, extracting even the marrow from the bones.

"For some days afterwards, I wandered through the woods. Unfortunately, I met my wife and children. I said to them that my son had died of starvation but I noticed immediately that they suspected the frightening reality.

"They then told me that they had not seen either my mother or brother. No doubt both had died of starvation, otherwise they would have been heard of, as it is now seven months since then. Three days after joining my family, the oldest of my boys died. We dug a grave with an axe and buried him. We were then reduced to boiling some pieces of our leather tent, our shoes and buffalo robes, in order to keep ourselves alive.

"I discovered that my family wanted to leave me from fear of meeting the same fate as my boy. One morning I got up early, and I don't know why — I was mad. It seems to me that all the devils had entered my heart. My wife and children were asleep around me. Pushed by the evil spirit, I took my gun, and placing the muzzle against her, shot her. I then without delay took my hatchet and massacred my three little girls. There was now but one little boy, seven years old, surviving. I awoke him and told him to melt some snow for water at once. The poor child was so weakened by long fasting to make any reflection of the frightful spectacle under his eyes. I took the bodies of my little girls and cut them up. I did the same with the corpse of my wife. I broke the skulls and took out the brains, and broke up the bones in order to get the marrow. My little son and I lived for seven or eight days on the flesh — I eating the flesh of my wife and children, he the flesh of his mother and sisters.

"At length I left there all the bones and started with the last of my family. Snow began to melt now. Spring had commenced. Ducks arrived and flew every day around us, and I could find enough to live upon, but I felt reluctant to see people. I then told my son that after some days we would meet people; they will know very soon that I am a murderer, and they will certainly make me die. As to you there is no fear; say all you know; no harm will be done to you. One day I had killed many ducks. I was a few miles from Egg Lake, where some relations of mine lived. I was sitting at the camp fire, when I told my son to go and fetch something five or six paces off. At that moment the devil suddenly took possession of my soul; and in order to live longer far from people, and to put out of the way the only witness to my crimes, I seized my gun and killed the last of my children and ate him as I did the others. Some weeks after I was taken by the police, sentenced to death, and in three days I am to be hanged."

Swift Runner's story, as told to Father Leduc, cleared up one mystery

Sergeant F. A. Bagley, in charge of Swift Runner's execution, was the youngest member of the NWMP during the 1874 trek. (See page 4.)

for the police. Ten people had gone into the woods that winter and only one had come out alive. However, only eight skulls had been found at the "starvation camp," leaving one person unaccounted for. The gruesome account of the last child's death was the missing link, for, despite what he confessed to Father Leduc, Swift Runner had already admitted to the police that he had killed and eaten his brother and his mother, who, he said ruefully, had been a bit tough!

With his confession, Swift Runner became a changed man. Ween-de-go no longer tormented him. He felt ready to embrace the faith of the Fathers who had befriended him at St. Albert Mission and made whatever peace he could with man and the white man's God.

The execution of Swift Runner presented special problems. To the Indians and many of the halfbreeds in the district, hanging was particularly disagreeable. They believed it "a death fit only for a dog." They believed, too, that hanging consisted of lifting a body up, holding it there and cutting it to pieces. Even Swift Runner, a big man, is said to have made merry at the thought of the hangman lifting him up to the rope.

Sheriff Richards, who lived at Battleford, made the long journey overland in the dead of winter for the execution. Because of the uncertainty of the trails, he telegraphed instructions to Colonel Jarvis to make the preparations and, if necessary, proceed with the execution as an example of police efficiency whether or not he had arrived. He reached Fort Saskatchewan on the evening of December 19, just in time to read the death warrant to the condemned man. Swift Runner received this news with a smile.

The morning of the execution dawned clear, with the temperature at 42 degrees below zero. Sergeant Fred Bagley, who had come west with the Force on its original march, was in charge of execution detail. At first no one would act as executioner and it appeared that Sheriff Richards would have to perform the melancholy function himself. But at the last moment, an old army pensioner named Rogers agreed to act.

Though Swift Runner had ignored the banging of the fort's carpenter as the scaffold was being constructed outside the guardroom, he examined it with great interest as he was led from his cell just after ten in the morning.

When placed on the trap, Swift Runner paid little heed as Rogers strapped his arms and legs. Instead he launched into a speech thanking the police for their kindness and the Fathers for their mercy. To the fifty or so spectators gathered for the West's first execution he reiterated that he knew he had done wrong. As he finished speaking, he shivered in the cold and, turning to the executioner, began to scold him for keeping him waiting so long in the chill air.

The groan of the trap door and the "swack" of the hangman's noose cut short his scolding. Swift Runner plunged through the opening and died instantly — the first person legally executed under the jurisdiction of the North-West Mounted Police.

"It was," summarized Jim Reade, one of the onlookers and a veteran of the California gold rush of 1849, "the purtiest hangin' I ever seen and it's the twenty-ninth."

Shoot-Out at New Hazelton

Hollywood couldn't have designed a better set or chosen finer actors to play this 1914 Western drama in the B.C. frontier community of New Hazelton. Led by the Reverend D. R. "Doc" McLean who was an expert with both bible and rifle, citizens shot it out with seven armed men who were robbing a bank.

Doc McLean
at New Hazelton
in 1914.

Two bandits lie dead on the wooden sidewalk near the bank. Inside the tent-cabin was another robber, shot in the hip. He died the next day.

During construction of the Grand Trunk Pacific Railway westward from Winnipeg across Saskatchewan, Alberta and British Columbia from 1906-14 scores of new communities were born. While several such as Prince George and Prince Rupert grew into cities, others flourished only during construction days then waned and survived as hamlets. Among the latter is New Hazelton some 290 km (180 miles) from Prince Rupert, the railway's western terminus on the Pacific. Its setting along Highway 16 amid B.C.'s snow-capped Coast Mountains is picturesque and peaceful, although this peacefulness has not always prevailed. In fact on the morning of April 7, 1914, New Hazelton's main street resembled a Wild West movie set, except that the hundreds of zinging bullets were as real as the robbers who dropped dead. And in the tradition of the Western movie the hero was a quiet spoken, unassuming man — the Reverend Donald Redmond McLean.

To every man, women and child in the little community, however, he was simply "Doc" and he was easy to recognize. He was muscular, well over six feet with curly black hair and a pleasant smile. In his western style hat and high, elk-hide boots he could have been likened perhaps to Gary

45

The town pump at New Hazelton where Doc was going for water when the robbery began. The photo below shows New Hazelton during railway construction days. After the railway was completed the community, like many others along the line, virtually disappeared.

Cooper, except that Cooper at the time was a thirteen-year-old Montana schoolboy.

Doc was a Nova Scotian by birth and had graduated from Knox College, Dalhousie University and Ontario Veterinary College. Few New Hazelton residents, however, knew of his academic background. He was more familiar to them as the man who preached on Sunday in a room above the drug store, and during the rest of the week was a social service worker among the construction crews and veterinarian for railway contractors Foley, Welch and Stewart. His love of animals was proverbial. In addition to caring for the hundreds of horses used during railway construction he always had time to tend a sick dog or other domestic pet. His main hobbies were hunting and fishing, and he was particularly fond of his British army Lee-Enfield .303 rifle.

At 10:15 on that April morning he walked peacefully up New Hazelton's main street, bucket in hand, toward the community's water pump. As he strolled along the dusty street he little realized that he was about to exchange the water bucket for his rifle, a weapon he handled as skillfully as the bible.

At the same time Al Gaslin, New Hazelton's postmaster who doubled as manager of Lynch's Hardware Store, was in the little log building that served as a branch of the Union Bank of Canada. "Going to be quiet around here from now on," he said to teller Bob Bishop, basing his prediction on the fact that construction of the Grand Trunk Pacific Railway was nearing completion.

In Gaslin's hand as he spoke were $50 in bills, a few cheques and his deposit slip. But before teller Bishop could take the money there came a diversion in the shape of more customers. There were six of them, roughly dressed in mackinaws and work pants, all unshaven, hard-eyed.

They weren't depositors, these six. They were bent on withdrawing. In addition, a rifle, carelessly cradled under one man's arm, and revolvers in the hands of his five companions suggested they were going to dispense with the usual bookkeeping formalities.

"Get your hands in the air. This is a holdup!" said their leader in a guttural sort of English. Bishop and his fellow bank employee, Reay Fenton, raised their hands in wonderment. As they did they saw through the shoulder-high front window another gang member outside on the sidewalk acting as lookout. Then the man with the rifle deftly removed the deposit from Gaslin's slightly quivering hand.

"Hey, don't take those cheques. They're no good to you," said the postmaster.

With a leer the bandit slipped the money into his pocket. Then he gave one or two quick commands (in Russian, as it turned out) and two of the gunmen stepped behind the counter and started cleaning out the cash drawers.

This wasn't Reay Fenton's first experience of a bank holdup, or the first one in these premises. Just six months before the same bank had been held up by just such another armed gang, also Russians. They had escaped with $17,000 and had shot teller Jock McQueen in the head, nearly killing him. As Fenton stood with his hands above his head he wondered if he or any of the others would be shot. Then he had an idea. There was a loaded gun in his bedroom at the rear of the building. Maybe he could make it?

With a quick turn he dashed through the rear door, got his hands on the gun, then whipped around to find the doorway blocked by one of the bank robbers. But at the sight of the resolute bank man, gun in hand, the bandit's courage evaporated. Slowly he stepped back from the door into the office.

It was lucky he didn't notice that almost inaudible click. It was Fenton's gun . . . and it had misfired.

Fenton slammed the door shut, and pulled his bed against it as a barrier. It was a courageous act and not in his bank contract. If he had wounded or killed the robber, the five others in the bank would probably have slaughtered him.

Meanwhile, in the outer office the gang was trying, in broken English, to get Bishop to open the safe. After the previous holdup the bank had replaced a wooden repository with a steel safe. It opened on a combination known only to Manager Tatchell, who hadn't come in yet, but was due any minute. Bishop tried to explain as best he could to the gun-waving gang leader.

Out on Pugsley Street, the muddy rutted cart track that fronted the bank, was the usual morning quiet. So far no one in the town suspected anything amiss at the bank. The unshaven lookout man in his work clothes resembled any other construction laborer waiting for a friend in the bank. After all, the town was full of foreigners, at least fifty of them Russians.

The first of the bank robbers to fall during the shoot-out with enraged citizens of New Hazelton.

Only difference, the man outside the bank was holding a Winchester rifle under his mackinaw.

Inside the bank the cash drawers had been looted of some $1,300 and in one corner Gaslin was still trying to argue the gang out of keeping his cheques. Across the room Bishop was being threatened with instant death if he didn't open the safe. Finally in exasperation, the gunman fired a succession of pistol shots around Bishop's feet.

"You fool!" snapped one of the robbers in English. "You'll have the whole town in here!" Bishop could see the shooting had made the gang uneasy, and a couple of them moved over to the window and glanced up and down the street.

New Hazelton, 6.5 km (4 miles) from Hazelton, was a boom creation of the Grand Trunk Railway construction. The old town, lying at the junction of the Skeena and Bulkley, had been in existence since the 1860s as a fur trading post in the heart of a vast trapping empire. Now the big railway construction job was drawing to a close, and soon trains from the east would cross northern B.C. to a Pacific terminus at Prince Rupert.

The business section of New Hazelton was typical boom town — a couple of streets lined with false front frame buildings that served as hotels, saloons, hardware store and other businesses. Further out was a clutter of shacks, a few acres of stumps and then the woods. The "avenues" crossing Pugsley were numbered but that was mostly for the benefit of the townsite promoters. By the time anyone reached 13th Avenue there was a good chance of encountering a bear rather than another resident.

The two robbers peering out of the bank's window weren't, however, concerned about the town's geography. Nor were they concerned about Doc, who was striding toward the town pump, bucket in hand, returning the morning greetings of the town's habitual loafers, both Indian and white. Then he fell in step with E.B. Tatchell, the new bank manager who had just been transferred from Prince Rupert. As they walked they were suddenly conscious of an odd noise up the street near the bank.

"Sounded like shots, Doc," said Tatchell. Then his eye caught the figure idling outside the bank. And something else. The idler was slipping a rifle out from under his mackinaw.

"It's a holdup, Doc," said Tatchell, grabbing his companion's arm. "Over at the bank!"

Preacher McLean tossed aside his bucket and started running — back to the tent that served as temporary accommodation. Tatchell was right at his heels. McLean secured his Lee-Enfield in a matter of seconds, and Mrs. McLean, with true frontier thoughtfulness, handed Tatchell her husband's .44 revolver.

As the two men raced back along Pugsley Street, restaurant owner Harry Lewis, who slapped bacon and beans in front of customers for a $1 a plate, ran across their path to disappear into his place of business. Seconds later he appeared, gun in hand.

The sole B.C. Police Officer for the district was at Hazelton. So was the magistrate, Allison. But these northerners were self-sufficient. And their civic pride had been hurt six months before when the bank was cleaned out under their noses and young Jock McQueen badly hurt. This time it was going to be different. The robbers would not be the only ones shooting.

"Open season on bank robbers!" yelled Harry Summer as, pistol in hand, he ducked from the side of a building to a better vantage point across the street.

The rifleman in the mackinaw outside the bank had now fired a couple of shots down Pugsley Street. As Doc McLean jogged along, gun in hand, a fistful of shells in his pocket, he ducked occasionally from doorway to doorway until he got to an intersection 55 m. (180 ft.) or so from the bank. There he spotted a pile of ore, dumped on the street by the Silver Standard Mine to exhibit their rich proposition.

Preacher McLean eyed the rockpile, then the menacing rifleman at the bank. With something between a leap and a slide he made it. Crouching behind the ore he was just in time to see the bank doors burst open and disgorge six armed men.

They hadn't come out at the first shots in the street because of

The bank, its front window bullet shattered, after the shoot-out.

confusion in the bank. Some were for staying indoors and making a stand, others wanted to get outside and retreat to the bush.

Finally, they reached the decision to get out on the street. Just as they did the lookout man leveled his Winchester at the preacher's head and shoulders visible behind the ore pile. The bandit's bullet ricocheted on the rocks alongside McLean's face to wail into space.

McLean's reaction was to spread a little flatter behind the ore as he worked the bolt of his .303 and with studied care lined up the sights. The rifleman at the bank didn't get off a second shot. He spun slowly and collapsed on the sidewalk.

The shooting intensified as more citizens joined from various vantage points along the street and from behind stumps. McLean, in a sideways glance, saw Bert Taylor in action, along with a man called Meagher. Then B.A. "Arizona" Smith, who ran one of the hotels, made a flying leap for the rockpile from some store doorway. In quick time Arizona's lever-action Winchester was keeping McLean company.

In the first exchange of shots a bullet had plunked through the upper window of the barber shop, where a lone customer was getting a shave. The smashing of the glass was the cue for him to wrench the sheet from his neck and drop to the floor. Somewhere he managed to get a rifle, for he was seen later hugging a nearby door post, one side of his face still lathered, a rifle butt pressing the other.

The bank robbers retreated slowly, keeping up a steady fire. As a result Doc McLean and his companion behind the ore pile were exposed to more than their share of the barrage from one rifle and five pistols.

But pistols and carbines couldn't outrange Doc McLean's Lee-Enfield. One of the gunmen, while making a grab for the lookout man's Winchester, fell victim to the preacher's unerring fire. He pitched forward with a broken leg, the weapon he wanted still out of his reach. Close behind him, a fellow gangster who had been blasting away steadily with a pistol was Doc's next target. The Russian suddenly found himself on his back, shoulder smashed. McLean seemed the coolest person on the street, despite the whining slugs that threatened momentarily to close his preacher-veterinarian career.

Two captured robbers, Boris Manukoff, left, and Zarachmet Kalaeff.

As a bullet spattered McLean's face with knife-edged rock particles, unflinchingly he squeezed off another round that toppled a fourth Russian. In a matter of a minute or so, six of the Russians were strewn along the road or the sidewalk. Two of them hadn't moved since they were hit, three moved spasmodically and one crawled slowly to seek sanctuary under the flap of an unoccupied tent pitched opposite the bank.

Only the seventh robber was still on his feet, retreating to the woods. As he reached the scrub he fired his last defiant shot. Then, whirling, disappeared into the bush.

The armed citizenry came from their places of concealment, most of them out of ammunition for over 500 shots had been exchanged in the brief battle. Two of the robbers were dead on the sidewalk outside the bank, but three others sprawled on the street were still alive, as was the man pulled out of the tent. He had been shot in the hip. The injured were given first aid, then moved to the hospital. The man with the smashed hip died the next day, but recovered consciousness long enough to give his name, Wano Dzntzoff.

The two men killed outside the bank were identified as Mischa Merzakoff and Obysel Borsaeff. Those who were alive were Borin Manukoff, Adeku Smajloff and Zarachmet Kalaeff. From the wounded men came the information that the man who disappeared in the bush was their leader, Dzachot Bekuzaroff. He had all the bank's money.

By the bloodstained trail it was evident that he had been hit but repeated search failed to reveal any trace of him.

The last shot fired in the battle of New Hazelton almost spelt tragedy for cashier Reay Fenton. As the excited mob of citizens approached the bank after the shooting was over, Fenton, Bishop and Gaslin came out the door. Fenton, in the lead, was just in time to get part of a blast from a shotgun in the hands of a trigger happy storekeeper. Luckily, the bank man was barely within range and got only a few pellets in his scalp as he ducked.

The police were summoned, and a month later the three Russian prisoners came up before Judge Young to get twenty years each.

In the weeks that followed their arrest, and as the wounded bank robbers made steady recovery, they told B.C. Police Officers Owen and Gammon, who came in from Prince Rupert and Hazelton to handle the investigation, a wild and dramatic story of the gang's background.

All were Russians, most from Siberia, members of a lawless sect feared even in that wilderness of swamp and frozen tundra. Bekuzaroff, the leader in the bank raid, had been a sort of outlaw chief in eastern Russia until action by the Czar's government sentenced him and his band to different forms of penal servitude. By superhuman effort some of them escaped, and Bekuzaroff, banished to the rock quarries of Sakhalin Island north of Japan, found himself released one day by lucky chance.

It appears that the end of the Russian-Japanese war saw part of the islands ceded to Japan by the Treaty of Portsmouth, and the Russian prisoners were free. Then along came an American schooner recruiting labor for construction of a railway in Mexico. From Mexico, Bekuzaroff worked his way up to San Francisco, and later to Vancouver, B.C. In

Mr. and Mrs. McLean in 1971 when they celebrated their diamond wedding anniversary. Mrs. McLean watched the shoot-out from a stump about a block from the ore pile where her husband and his rifle were bowling over the bank robbers.

Doc in the Cariboo in 1927 when he had changed careers and become a school teacher.

Vancouver the bank robbery was planned, and the rest of the gang was picked up along the line of railway construction in Northern B.C.

The only thing the gang hadn't anticipated was New Hazelton's community spirit, and the imperturbable preacher, Doc McLean.

There were two aftermaths to the shooting affray. A year later, a stranger, obviously Russian, appeared in New Hazelton and made some enquiries as to the whereabouts of Doc McLean. Townsmen figured from the stranger's conversation that he was a brother of one of the dead bandits and might be on revenge. The police, called over from Hazelton, interrogated the stranger. As he couldn't give a satisfactory account of himself he was ordered out of town on the next train.

Just to see that nothing unusual happened during the stranger's stay in town, a citizen stayed with him wherever he went, all day long. For complete security, the citizen packed a Winchester.

If the stranger bought tobacco, his guard went with him, ostentatiously slapping the carbine on the counter before him. That evening when the visitor was escorted to the train, the police at Prince Rupert were advised by wire. There they checked him off the train onto a southbound boat. Ultimately he arrived in Vancouver, never to be heard of again.

It all sounds rather melodramatic, but it shows what the citizens thought of Doc McLean.

Months after the bank robbery came word from the Union Bank's head office of a reward. Suggestion was made that some of those concerned should be given gold watches suitably inscribed. Or, in the alternative, $100 cash. There were knowing looks as the participants voted for the cash. The upshot was the biggest stag party ever held between the Panama Canal and the Arctic Circle, a blowout that was the topic of conversation for years.

With the completion of the railway ending his work in New Hazelton, Doc and his family left in 1915. He moved to Quesnel in the Cariboo where he continued his church work and attending to sick animals. From Quesnel his work took him to Cloverdale and Powell River but in 1925 he changed careers and became a teacher. He returned to the Cariboo and taught at Quesnel for two years, then moved to Burnaby and taught for twenty years until his retirement in 1947. But though retired, he continued as a relief teacher for ten more years.

Doc died at Port Moody in 1975, a distinguished man of ninety-five. Although he had been a minister, veterinarian and a school principal he is best remembered as a marksman since the New Hazelton shoot-out has become a northern legend.

"Dad never looked upon himself as a gun slicker," recalls one of his four daughters, Mrs. Margaret Greenwood. "Nor was he and the other citizens trying to be heroes and save the bank's money. They were up in arms because of the robbery six months before, probably by the same bunch, and the shooting of Jock McQueen in the face. They were determined to protect townspeople from a similar incident."

That they succeeded is evident from the fact that of the seven bandits, six were captured or killed.

Death of Manitoba's Pioneer Police Chief

Reproduction of an 1873 painting by E. J. Hutchins showing Winnipeg and Fort Garry.

The Manitoba Provincial Police was formed in October 1870 shortly after the province's entry into Canada. Under the leadership of Captain John Villiers, assisted by Louis de Plainval, nineteen men were sworn in, issued with a miscellany of weapons and nondescript uniforms, and posted throughout the thinly populated region. Nineteen-year-old Richard Power was one of the original members.

Within two years, few originals remained. While most of the men resigned to accept positions in the rapidly expanding business world of Winnipeg, one was dismissed for drunkeness and striking his superior

In 1874 twenty-three-year-old Richard Power became Manitoba's Chief Constable. He was soon well known for both his courage and a huge Colt .45 with a nine-inch barrel.

officer and another received a five-year sentence for the shooting death of a young soldier at Fort Garry barracks. Even Richard Power narrowly escaped dismissal for shooting an Indian during an arrest.

As officers resigned or were dismissed, they were not replaced and the force shrank from nineteen to a pathetic eight-man squad. Partly as a result of this rapid depletion, but more because of his ability for police work, Power was promoted rapidly until February 1874 when he was appointed Chief Constable at the age of twenty-three.

Just before his appointment Winnipeg had incorporated as a city and created its own small police force under John S. Ingram. Power, now responsible for policing the province except for Winnipeg, revamped his force by stationing men at posts such as Selkirk, Kildonan and St. Norbert

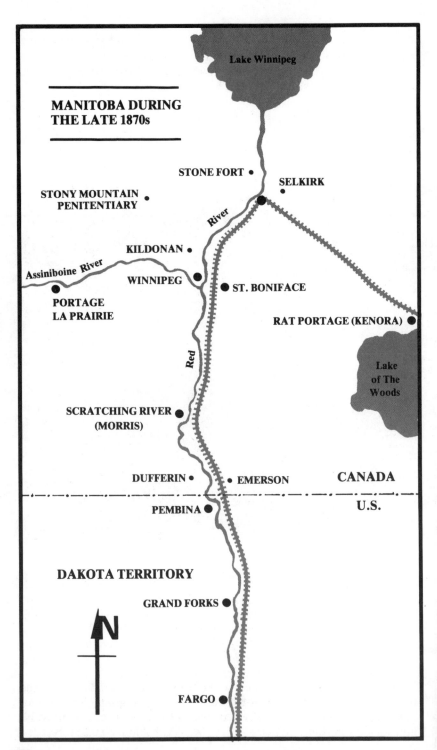

MANITOBA DURING THE LATE 1870s

Lake Winnipeg

STONE FORT

SELKIRK

STONY MOUNTAIN PENITENTIARY

River

KILDONAN

Assiniboine River

WINNIPEG

ST. BONIFACE

PORTAGE LA PRAIRIE

RAT PORTAGE (KENORA)

Red

Lake of The Woods

SCRATCHING RIVER (MORRIS)

DUFFERIN

EMERSON

CANADA

U.S.

PEMBINA

DAKOTA TERRITORY

GRAND FORKS

N

FARGO

outside the city but where the population was concentrated. His head-quarters were in a log building just off Winnipeg's Main Street and here he stationed the remainder of his small force. Law enforcement at places like Portage la Prairie and Emerson had to depend on vigilantes and volunteer police.

Across the Canadian-American border in neighboring Dakota Territory law enforcement officers were even fewer. There was only one officer, Sheriff Brown, at Pembina, with the nearest help some distance away at Fargo. As a consequence, so long as outlaws stayed away from the few populated centers, they could operate with impunity.

Among these outlaws was Edward Couture who headed a gang from a hideout south of Pembina. Their method was to make quick midnight horse raids on the farms of Manitoba settlers and scamper back before the Manitoba Provincial Police arrived. The stolen horses were then driven deep into Dakota Territory and sold.

Chief Constable Power's involvement with the gang was the result of a telegram from F.T. Bradley, Customs Officer and Justice of the Peace at the border village of Emerson. He advised that one of Couture's gang, Edward Martin, was heading north to visit relatives. As dawn broke over Winnipeg on September 7, 1874, Power and a constable named Heusens saddled up and rode south along the stagecoach road to the twin border villages of Emerson and Pembina. Subsequent events were an indication of Power's courage, tenacity and luck, since he should have died during his first encounter with Martin. The events also demonstrated that Martin could break from prison as easily as he stole a horse.

It was a 70-km (43-mile) ride from Winnipeg to the stagecoach station at Scratching River (Morris) where Power planned to lie in wait for the horse thief. Darkness had fallen when the lawmen arrived within sight of the stopping place. They left their horses with a nearby settler and approached on foot. Moments later two horsemen rode in from the south. It was Edward Martin and a fellow outlaw, Charles Garden.

Power noted that the horse Martin was riding resembled the description of one stolen the previous month. He stepped forward and seized the bridle. At the same time, Heusens grasped Garden by the pant leg. Ordered to dismount, the two men got down quietly.

As it was too dark to return to Winnipeg, Power decided to keep his prisoners, who were not considered dangerous, at the stagecoach station for the night and start early the following morning. He walked Martin forward while Heusens remained with Garden to care for the horses. As they passed through the entrance to the station, Martin lunged at Power, throwing him off balance. Before the officer could recover, Martin drew a revolver and fired at point-blank range. His first shot missed. As he swung round for a second, Power recovered his balance and grappled with him in the room.

Heusens and Garden, hearing the shot, started for the station — but with different intentions. Heeding a shout from Martin, Garden sprang into the room and swept a coal-oil lamp from the table, plunging the room into darkness. He then drew a hunting knife from his boot and flung himself on Constable Heusens. That was a mistake. Heusens stood door high and was a hefty mass of muscle and bone. With a sweep of his hand he bounced Garden off the nearest wall and leaped to Power's assistance. Meanwhile, Martin had managed to get his finger on the trigger and fired a couple of random shots. Garden did not appreciate the flying bullets and scrambled for the door.

Power broke loose from Martin, pulled his Colt .45 — the largest model made with a nine-inch barrel — and ordered Martin to drop his gun. The outlaw complied meekly. Leaving Heusens to guard him, Power started in pursuit of Garden. A noise sent him in the direction of the corral where he glimpsed a figure sprinting into the darkness. Power fired and heard a muffled cry, but it was too dark to investigate and he returned to the station.

The following morning Power found traces of blood near the corral and realized that he had hit Garden. Ordering Heusens to escort Martin to the prison in Winnipeg, he saddled his horse and began tracking the escapee. His job was made easier when a settler brought word that Garden was in his shack, seeking refuge with a leg wound. Power quickly arrested him and with a borrowed team and wagon took him to Winnipeg. Here he was given medical attention and jailed — but only for a short time.

At 11 o'clock on the night of October 1, Constable Heusens made the rounds of the prison. He checked each prisoner through a peephole in the cell door, noted that all was in order and went back to the office. Heusens was relieved at midnight by another constable. On making his inspection he noticed that prisoner Charles Bigeral's cell door was not closed tight and that the "figure" lying on the bunk was a dummy. A quick check of

other cell doors revealed that all were locked except Edward Martin's, whose bunk also contained a roll of blankets made to look like a sleeping man. Garden, Martin's partner, still slumbered peacefully in his cell.

Undetected, Martin and Bigeral had picked five locks from the cell door to the corridor, then to the central square where they had opened and relocked doors leading to the center hall. Here, without being seen, they picked the massive lock on the door and walked into the street.

There was no telephone in the prison and the solitary guard spent considerable time finding someone to alert Chief Constable Power. It was nearly morning before a pursuit was organized. Power suspected that a gang member named Rogers was an accomplice since he had been seen in the vicinity of the prison on several occasions following Martin's arrest. He also believed — correctly as events proved — that Rogers had met the escapees outside the prison with horses and a change of clothing.

After meeting Rogers the fugitives rode south across the border where Bigeral parted from Martin and Rogers. Freedom for the latter two was short, however. In response to telegraphic warnings by Power to sheriffs in Dakota and Minnesota, they were captured near Glyndon, Minnesota, on October 23. With them were five stolen horses.

Martin was jailed at Moorhead (North Dakota) to await trial for possession of stolen property and possible extradition to Manitoba. The warden, aware of his ability to pick locks, placed him in leg irons and added a second lock to the cell door. Martin bided his time. On May 5, 1875, Martin picked both locks then released his leg irons with a key from the sheriff's office. There were too many people on the street to risk

Winnipeg's Main Street in 1880 and, opposite page, Portage la Prairie in the same year. Because of the shortage of policemen, Portage la Prairie relied on a local vigilante committee to keep order.

walking out, so he bored a hole through the side wall of the office and let himself into the space between the jail and an adjacent building.

Martin was next reported at Cheyenne where he stole a boat and headed for the Canadian border. A few days later he was captured at Sioux Falls with two stolen horses. Under heavy guard he was taken to Fargo and sentenced to serve a severe term in the territorial prison. From here he did not escape. On release he was believed to have headed west for the more hospitable climes of Montana Territory.

The remainder of the horse thieves were rounded up, either by Power and the Manitoba Provincial Police or Dakota authorities. The leader, Edward Couture, was brought to trial in Winnipeg on June 14, 1875. He was charged with sixteen counts of horse theft but his lawyers managed to get a four month postponement. Couture never came to trial since he also escaped from the Winnipeg prison and headed south, although his arrest did break up the gang.

But tracking horse thieves and chasing prison escapees were only part of Chief Constable Power's duties. He was, for instance, involved in several murder cases. His first major case was that of Joseph Michaud who was hanged in public in 1874 for murdering James R. Brown. Then followed the conviction of Gilbert Godon for slaying Benjamin Marchand.

In 1875 Power was confronted by two murders. On May 3, the body of John O'Maley was discovered in a small stream near the border, the motive apparently $1,000 O'Maley had in his possession. Two weeks later Power was presented with a second body from the same river. Like O'Maley, the man had been shot several times, wrapped in heavy chains and dumped in the river. Despite a thorough investigation of the twin murders, no one was ever brought to trial.

Power was more successful in the spring of 1878 when he and a posse captured killer John Gribbon. Gribbon was convicted of manslaughter but he, too, escaped from jail and crossed into the U.S. He was later arrested by U.S. authorities then released in November 1879 on a legal technicality. Re-arrested the following day at the urging of Chief Power for the suspected murder of two women several years before, Gribbon was again set free when Power was not given time to prepare a strong enough case.

A few months later Power was involved with another prison escapee — Edward Daniels. This encounter was nearly fatal for Power and he escaped death only because Daniels' revolver failed to fire.

The case of Edward Daniels began on June 16, 1875, when he was sentenced to two years for stealing from a Winnipeg store. He was sent to the provincial penitentiary, issued with the number 21 and a two-color prison suit of clothes (the left half grey, the right half blue). His prison stay also was brief. On the afternoon of September 18, a small group of men, including Daniels, were working in the prison yard under surveillance of a solitary guard. One prisoner on the roof called for instructions. The guard shouted back but the inmate protested that he did not understand, forcing the guard to climb the ladder. When the guard returned, Daniels was missing.

It was later learned from Daniels' diary that the night after his escape he burgled the home of Captain Kennedy, a justice of the peace, for whom he once worked. He helped himself to provisions and clothing before making his way to Winnipeg where he stole a horse and buggy and by back roads crossed the border into Dakota. His first stop was Deadwood where, using the name William Chiraton, he posed as a freighter from Manitoba. At that time, Deadwood was a hangout for notorious gamblers such as Wild Bill Hickok, as well as gunmen, whiskey traders and goldseekers. Daniels recorded in his diary that twice he was involved in gun fights but managed to escape both times. Since the diary was for Daniels own use it is unlikely that he invented these incidents.

The following autumn, still using the name Chiraton, he returned to Manitoba, again burgling Captain Kennedy's home. He outfitted himself with food and clothing, then burgled several other homes in the area before moving east. He went into hiding by hiring on as a construction worker on the Canadian Pacific Railway.

But Winnipeg seemed to fascinate him and in October 1876 he was back. This time, however, he spared the unfortunate Captain Kennedy by stealing a horse from a Mr. Campbell. He hid the animal in the woods and returned, but this time was seen boldly leading a horse from Reverend Matheson's stable. Daniels managed to escape before the police arrived.

Chief Constable Richard Power doggedly followed his man from farm to farm along the stagecoach road to Emerson. He found Campbell's horse at a settler's farm and was told that Daniels had also sold him a horse the previous year. Power inspected the animal and confirmed that it was one stolen from a resident of St. Andrews.

Learning that his man was only a few hours ahead, Power telegraphed Sheriff Brown at Pembina. Daniels was apprehended on October 25 as he rode into town on Reverend Matheson's horse. As a consequence, in June 1877 Edward Daniels was convicted of bringing stolen property into Dakota and sentenced to two years in Stillwater Territorial Penitentiary, largely on evidence provided by Power. The outlaw and the lawman, however, were not yet free of each other.

Daniels was released in 1879 and returned to Manitoba and his old way of life. Prison had made him more bitter and dangerous as was evident when he burgled the house of a Mrs. Ross. When she surprised him in the act Daniels showed her he was well armed and said he would kill the first man who tried to arrest him. As soon as her unwelcome visitor left, she hastened to Captain Kennedy who instructed Manitoba Police detectives Smith and Macdonald to bring in the outlaw, dead or alive.

Learning that Daniels was heading for St. Boniface, the two detectives went to a saloon owned by Louis Platcher, one of many who sympathized with Daniels. Although Daniels was warned that the detectives were waiting, he could not resist baiting them. Two nights later he walked into the saloon disguised in a woman's cloak and, as later learned, two revolvers thrust into his belt. After purchasing a bottle of whiskey within a few feet of the detectives he sauntered casually through the front entrance.

Despite the disguise, however, Daniels had been recognized by several people in the saloon. But they feared warning the detectives while he was still inside in case a shoot-out resulted. Once alerted, Smith and Macdonald gave chase, but Daniels eluded them in the dark. It was then he dropped his diary that recorded his adventures and crimes since escaping from the penitentiary in 1875.

Daniels crossed the border to Pembina where he joined a band of horse thieves. But within three months he was back in the Winnipeg area. For some strange reason, he seemed to take pleasure in stealing from the same people. Reverend Matheson's stable was revisited and the same horse stolen again. He next went to Mary Inkster's home where he helped himself to seven bottles of beer, despite the protests of that astonished lady.

In response to Mrs. Inkster's call for help, a posse of six men assembled in her yard, but their enthusiasm waned on learning that Daniels was armed with two revolvers. They were still debating a judicious course when Chief Constable Power rode up with special constable Sam Gerrard.

Under Power's direction the posse scoured the area. Two encountered Daniels as he was about to enter another settler's house, but not wishing to tangle with the outlaw, they rode in search of Chief Power. Daniels had left on Reverend Matheson's horse long before either Power or Gerrard reached the scene.

The search continued through the night without success. Then at 10 o'clock next morning Power received an astonishing message. The young criminal was at a farmstead — cutting the grass. But the driveway to the place offered no concealment and Daniels easily recognized the approaching Power. In seconds he was headed for the nearest woods astride the unfortunate Matheson horse.

Instead of chasing Daniels, Power changed tactics. He left the Kildonan area, stating that he had received word that Daniels was in another part of the province. He counted on this message being relayed to Daniels and hoped that the outlaw's daring and bravado would lead him into an error of judgement. Power was not disappointed.

Manitoba Provincial Policemen at
Rat Portage in the early 1880s.

Early Wednesday morning, two men brought word that Daniels was staying the night with a friend in St. Paul's. Stationing Gerrard outside the bedroom window, Power entered the house and carefully eased open the bedroom door. Despite the stealth and caution, Daniels was alert. As Power stepped into the room, gun drawn, the outlaw raised his revolver and pulled the trigger. There was a click but no flash of flame. The gun had misfired, saving Power from almost certain death. Daniels hurled the useless weapon aside and dived for a second revolver on the bed.

With incredible fortitude, Chief Constable Power refrained from shooting the trapped man. As Daniels whirled with the second gun in hand, he found himself looking down the muzzle of Power's massive .45. He dropped his revolver and backed away.

Handcuffed and shackled, Daniels was taken to the provincial jail at Winnipeg. Despite the fact that he was well known to Power, he said that his name was Frank Morris and that he had never heard of Edward Daniels. He maintained this subterfuge even when his aunt identified him. Only when the penitentiary warden advised him to admit his identity, return to the penitentiary and complete as much as possible of his original sentence before new ones were imposed, did Daniels relent.

Two months later, Edward Daniels was brought before Chief Justice Wood charged with a handful of offences dating back to the first theft of Reverend Matheson's horse in 1876. Convicted of some and acquitted of others for lack of evidence, he received sentences totalling fourteen years.

The jail at Rat Portage in the early 1880s.

Had his revolver not misfired, he could well have killed Power and been sentenced to hang.

Although Power escaped death while capturing both Daniels and Martin, he was not so fortunate in his next encounter with a fugitive.

Mike Carroll was one of those frontier types known as a "hard case." He drifted into the Thunder Bay area of Ontario in the mid 1880s, seeking employment on the Canadian Pacific Railway being built to Rat Portage (Kenora). His real talent, however, lay in picking pockets rather than driving spikes, with fellow workmen quickly relieved of their wallets.

Arrested for these relatively slight misdemeanours, Carroll was given a short sentence in the lockup at Rat Portage. Then authorities discovered that he had a long record in Eastern Canada that included an escape from Toronto's Central Prison, considered the ultimate in security. Carroll was also credited with several other prison breaks, and soon added Rat Portage's jail to his list.

Unfortunately for Carroll, he tended to be talkative. As a result, word soon reached Detective O'Keefe of the Manitoba Provincial Police that his man was at Selkirk, north of Winnipeg. He wired Detective Malcolm McKenzie at Cross Lake who caught the first train to Selkirk. Tracking his man to the hotel dining room, McKenzie invited him to hold out his wrists for handcuffs. Instead, Carroll shoved a table into McKenzie's stomach and darted through the door. Like most Manitoba policemen, McKenzie had been selected for size rather than for speed and the ensuing footrace was no contest. The frustrated detective sent several bullets after the fleet little outlaw, but Carroll escaped into the darkness.

Fortunately for the police, Carroll still hadn't learned the value of silence. He could not resist bragging about his escapade to a barber who passed the information to Power. The outlaw quickly found himself back in jail. This time he evidently had realized the value of silence for he remained quiet until Detective O'Keefe told him he planned to return him to Ontario to face prison breaking and other charges. If this transfer happened, Carroll threatened, he would drown the detective while crossing Lake of the Woods, even if he perished himself.

Despite the threat, on July 3, 1880, Carroll was escorted by Power and McKenzie to Rat Portage. Here he was found guilty by Magistrate C.J. Brereton and sentenced to two years. At that time, the territory around Rat Portage was a political wilderness, with magistrates having the option of sentencing prisoners to serve time either in Manitoba or Ontario. In Carroll's case, Brereton decided that Winnipeg's prison offered better security than Thunder Bay's lockup — especially in view of the man's history of escapes. He therefore ordered Detective O'Keefe to transport Carroll back to Manitoba.

Despite Carroll's threat to drown O'Keefe, the journey was accomplished successfully and he was jailed on July 8. But not for long. On July 23, Carroll was one of a group of prisoners cutting wood at the government offices on Main Street. The guard in charge had taken the precaution of asking for a ball and chain for Carroll, but this request was denied.

Later that day, a man in prison clothing was reported sprinting along

An 1879 sketch of the ferry at St. Boniface where Police Chief Power died on duty.

Main Street in the direction of a bridge being built across the Red River between Winnipeg and St. Boniface.

Chief Constable Power was in bed with fever when advised of Carroll's escape. He dressed, strapped on his Colt .45 and collected Constable J. Bell. Together they traced the escapee to the bridge which he had crossed in full view of the workmen. From there trailing the escapee was simple since Carroll had had to escape minus his shoes, a safety precaution on guard McKay's part. Several people had noticed a man carefully picking his way along the railway track south of St. Boniface.

The search ended at a haystack late that evening. Carroll, his feet cut and swollen, emerged and simply grinned in resignation when he saw the two policemen. Power commandeered a railway handcar and, with all three taking turns, pumped themselves back to St. Boniface.

They arrived at the village about midnight to find the ferry not running. However, a man with a rowboat offered to take them across. Power stepped into the boat first and turned to help his handcuffed prisoner. Carroll put his foot on the gunwale, whether by accident or design it was never revealed, and the boat overturned. Both men disappeared beneath the surface of the river.

In the darkness Bell and the boatman caught a glimpse of Carroll a few lengths downstream but Richard Power was never seen alive again. His body was found the next morning not far from the loading dock, weighed down by the ammunition belt and heavy Colt .45. Carroll's body was discovered some distance downstream. His earlier threat to drown O'Keefe led to speculation that the outlaw had deliberately upset the rowboat in order to escape.

The *Manitoba Daily Free Press* carried a full account of the tragedy in its July 28, 1880, edition, noting:

"The city was surprised and grieved this morning by the announcement that Richard Power, Chief of the Provincial Police, had been drowned during the night while attempting to cross the Red River with a prisoner — the notorious Mike Carroll. It seemed impossible to realize the fact that he, who was in our midst but yesterday in the prime of his vigor and manhood, had been thus suddenly cut off, even while in the active discharge of his duties."

An editorial in the same edition noted:

"By the untimely death of Mr. Richard Power . . . the Province loses, we believe, its oldest, and we are sure one of its most faithful and efficient officers. Mr. Power entered the public service at the very organization of the Province in the capacity of a mounted policeman, and has ever since been connected with the police, for the most of the time as chief. Fear was a quality which Mr. Power, it is said by those who knew him best, did not possess. His deeds of daring and intrepidity are numerous, and it was the prognostication of his aquaintances that he would certainly die on duty . . . ."

Constable Power was buried with full military honors, including a gun carriage to carry his body to the cemetery. During his funeral activity in the community virtually halted. As the newspaper noted: "His friends are numbered by hundreds . . . ."

Jingling Bells

For centuries in the West, Indians didn't consider snatching another man's horse as stealing. But as a brave with the colorful name of Jingling Bells learned, the NWMP didn't agree.

Since the art of lifting another man's transportation was practiced long before the coming of law and order to the Canadian West, it is unlikely that the name of the West's first horse thief will ever be known. In a culture where a woman could be purchased for a horse and where both wealth and prestige were measured to a great degree by the possession of ponies, horse stealing was an accepted practice.

A Blackfoot Indian camp on the prairie in 1883.
Horses were prized by the Indians as status symbols,
with a proficient horse thief earning great
respect from fellow tribesmen.

In 1879 Inspector Sam Steele of the North-West Mounted Police noted that "The Indian custom of buying wives was very much in evidence at this time; some of the younger squaws were held by their fathers at high prices, and one Saulteaux girl was valued at thirty horses, although the usual price or present was a rifle or one horse."

But while horse stealing might have been culturally acceptable to one class of society, it certainly wasn't to another — the animals' owners. For this reason those caught stealing horses tended to encounter justice that was swift and severe, especially south of the border. In June 1879 Inspector Steele was ordered to Bismarck, Dakota, to meet a party of police recruits who were coming West via the U.S. Because of rainstorms he was delayed at Fort Benton on the Upper Missouri River and later wrote: "Even in our day short shrift had been given to many a horse thief. There was a magistrate, a sheriff, and deputies, and unless the accused was a horse thief he would get a fair trial. Five years later, however, there were 40 genuine or alleged horse thieves hanged by the vigilantes . . . ."

(At Fort Benton's excellent museum visitors can see for themselves the quick justice given horse thieves. Among displays are a collection of headlines from newspapers of the frontier era. One records the fate of a

horse thief with the terse headline: "TELEGRAPHED HIM HOME." An equally terse sub-headline provides the following additional information: "Hanged Horse Thief With His Own Lariat to Western Union Pole.")

In Canada, William Martin was the first recorded horse thief after Manitoba entered into Confederation in 1870. Convicted of swiping several cayuses, Martin was sentenced to the Stone Fort Penitentiary but escaped from the local prison before being transferred. He was next heard from in Crookston, North Dakota, and an effort was made to extradite him. This attempt failed and Martin was released, a development which proved not in his best interest since he was later killed in a gun battle.

On the Western Plains, James Brooks, a fugitive from Montana, had the distinction of being the first horse thief convicted by the North-West Mounted Police. In 1876 he was sentenced to five years but as the nearest penitentiary was in Manitoba he had to travel nearly 1,300 km (800 miles) by horse across the prairies to his new home at Stony Mountain.

The most colorful of the early horse snatchers was a Blood Indian with an equally colorful name — Jingling Bells.

In August 1879 Jingling Bells showed up at the NWMP post at Fort Macleod. He was suspected of having killed a Cree Indian at Blackfoot Crossing, but nothing could be proved. A man with a mechanical turn of mind, Jingling Bells shortly got himself into difficulty through his passion for watches. When Constable Arnold McCauley missed his faithful time-piece, it coincided with Jingling Bells' delighted acquisition of an identical

Stone Fort Penitentiary. Before completion of the CPR in the early 1880s, prisoners from the West were transported 1,300 km (800 miles) by horses to jail.

watch. Brought before the magistrate, he received thirty days. That was on August 25, 1879.

Furthering his mechanical interest, Jingling Bells spent some time probing the mysteries of the locks on the leg-irons that he wore. Three days later he had the solutions. On August 28, while being escorted to the latrine, he suddenly threw his blanket over the policeman's head, opened the lock and fled. Though sentry Jack O'Neil fired several shots at him, Jingling Bells ran through the fort gate and disappeared into the timber.

While Jingling Bells' method of escaping his leg-irons was not solved, he did change police procedure. Officers thereafter poured melted lead into the key holes whenever they held a serious offender.

Jingling Bells remained at large for nearly a year. Then on July 16, 1880, Corporal Patterson was sent to the Blood reserve to investigate a case of theft. On arresting the culprit, he was surprised to find that it was Jingling Bells in disguise. Arraigned on the new charge on August 4, 1880, Jingling Bells was acquitted. For his previous offense of breaking jail in 1879, however, he was returned to the lock-up.

After serving his term, Jingling Bells abandoned his quest for watches and turned his talents to bigger quarry — unattended horses. In September 1881 with two Indian colleagues, Marrow Bones and The Only Wood, he stole not one horse but an entire herd from the Morley Indians near Banff and drove it south towards the American border. Unfortunately, while passing Fort Macleod NWMP post their noise alerted a night sentry and a patrol was sent out. The three were taken into custody.

On October 22, 1881, Jingling Bells received a severe three-year sentence in the penitentiary, Marrow Bones got eighteen months, while The Only Wood drew one year. Because winter was approaching, no effort was made to transport Jingling Bells the 1,300 km (800 miles) to Stony Mountain Penitentiary in Manitoba. He remained in the log prison at the police barracks with his two companions.

Though Jingling Bells vowed that he would not be taken to the "big prison," it was Marrow Bones who eventually escaped. When summer arrived and transportation became possible, the police, alert to a rumor that Marrow Bones was planning to ambush the police escort and free Jingling Bells, sent a wagon down the trail with a constable huddled under a blanket. When no attempt was made to waylay the decoy, Jingling Bells was taken out to rendezvous with a wagon far out on the trail.

The police escort was two weeks on the trail before reaching the head of the new Canadian Pacific Railway at Portage la Prairie. From here Jingling Bells was transported by the white man's "iron horse" to Stony Mountain and admitted on May 25, 1882.

Jingling Bells never left. He quickly succumbed to tuberculosis — a common ailment of Plains Indians in jail. But not only Jingling Bells had passed on. So had the centuries-old Indian philosophy that stealing horses was not really stealing. In the U.S. the rangeland vigilantes, and in Western Canada the Mounted Police, were powerful reasons for respecting other people's property. The consequence of ignoring these reasons ranged from being a guest at a necktie party to spending several uncomfortable years in jail.

The Dog and Big Rib

One of the great myths of the Wild West is that of the "gun-slinger," the expert marksman who could dot the "i" on a lawman's badge or plug a mosquito between the shoulder blades at twenty paces. If our great grandfathers had known how to shoot, the plains from Winnipeg to the Rockies would have been carpeted with corpses. As it was, the carpet was made largely of harmlessly expended bullets. But, they tried.

In late April 1887, a rancher named Watson who lived near Medicine Hat missed some of his horses and sent word to the North-West Mounted Police post at Maple Creek. In response Staff Sergeant Spicer, leading a small patrol, soon picked up tracks which led southward to the Cypress Hills. On April 25, a few kilometers south of Maple Creek, the police party was fired upon by a small band of Indians. A long-range gun battle took place but no one was injured and the Indians decamped.

A short time later, evidently hoping to add to its stock of stolen horses, the same raiding party swooped down on Urpin Station. Here they took several shots at a man named Adsit, but the raiders garnered neither steed nor scalp for their efforts.

A telegraph warning was sent to Fort Macleod and Sergeant-Major

These two Indians couldn't resist rounding up
unattended horses. Fortunately, irate owners didn't
catch them or, like the Montana horse thief in the previous
chapter, they may have been "Telegraphed home."

The photo at left shows Big Rib, in white blanket coat, after he had reformed and was a
NWMP scout during the 1896 hunt for a murderer named Charcoal. (See *Outlaws and
Lawmen of Western Canada,* Volume Two.)
Below is Dunmore Junction in 1886. In the upper left hand corner is the Ford Hotel from
which The Dog and Big Rib escaped.

Lake with a thirty-man patrol was ordered to scour the rolling hills
between Lethbridge and the Cypress Hills. It was suspected that the
raiders were American Indians and might be heading for the safety of the
Medicine Line, as the border was called by the Indians. Despite a thorough
search, no contact was made with the marauders. But Lake was able to
learn the name of two of them — The Dog and Big Rib, members of the
Mule Camp of Blood Indians near Fort Macleod.

A watch was kept on the camp and within three weeks Inspector
Sanders succeeded in arresting the two wanted men. They were brought
before Judge McLeod on May 17, 1887, and charged with attempted
murder. But the evidence was so scanty that the charge was withdrawn and
substituted with an indictment for the theft of Watson's horses. Both men
pleaded guilty.

In passing sentence, Judge McLeod remarked that he had in the past
been inclined to deal leniently with Indians but that his leniency had
evidently been mistaken for softness. He imposed a severe term of five
years for each.

As The Dog and Big Rib were escorted from the courthouse at Fort

Macleod their friends and relatives pushed forward and within minutes formed a shoving mass. Police reinforcements moved in to surround the prisoners who added to the confusion by dancing and chanting songs of defiance. It was an ugly situation, but the police slowly gained control and relentlessly pushed their charges along the street to the local guard room. As they approached the log prison an old woman, believing that death was better than dishonor, whipped a knife from beneath her shawl and tried to stab one of the captives.

Once the two Blood Indians were in the lock-up, the Mounted Police placed a strong guard over them and added extra outside patrols as the temperature of the Indians continued at fever level. However, by early evening the excitement abated and the night passed without incident. The following morning the two men were spirited out of town in charge of Sheriff Campbell and two escorts.

The first part of the 1,300-km (800-mile) journey from Fort Macleod to Stony Mountain Penitentiary at Winnipeg was by wagon to Lethbridge. Here the party switched to a quaint little coal company railroad nick-named "The Turkey Track." It ran at the breathtaking speed of 30 km (19 miles) an hour between Lethbridge and Dunmore Junction, with the train crew frequently stopping to visit local stockmen along the right-of-way.

Connections with the CPR main line passenger trains were normally made at Dunmore Junction, east of Medicine Hat. On this occasion, however, the east-bound train had been cancelled and the prisoners and escort stayed overnight in Dunmore. Shackling The Dog and Big Rib together, Sheriff Campbell locked them in a back room on the second storey of the Ford Hotel. With a guard posted in front of the door, Campbell retired for the night, confident that his prisoners were secure.

About 1 o'clock in the morning the guard checked the room. To his horror he discovered the prisoners gone. Even though shackled together they had managed to lower themselves some 4.5 m (15 ft.) from the window to the ground. The guard at once wakened Sheriff Campbell.

Campbell, believing that the escapees could not travel far at night in shackles, and noting that a rainstorm was making the black night even blacker, decided to take another short nap before setting off in pursuit. At dawn a search was instituted but there was no trace of the fugitives. Rain had wiped out all tracks. The Dog and Big Rib seemed to have disappear-ed down a gopher hole. In desperation, Campbell issued orders that they were to be taken dead or alive, but in spite of this drastic edict the two horse thieves remained at large.

That summer tension between Indians and settlers rose to its highest pitch since the Riel Rebellion of 1885. Within a week after the escape of The Dog and Big Rib, the body of Peter Smith, operator of a stopping house on the Qu'Appelle-Prince Albert stagecoach line, was found near Touchwood. Then on May 31, Hector McLeish, a settler near Qu'Appelle, was shot dead by two suspected half-breed horse thieves. Two days later Rory McLean, another settler, was shot to death on the Indian reservation near Whitewood. Within twenty-four hours, yet another homesteader, Samuel Poole, died of a bludgeoning.

By early June some 400 police and vigilantes were searching the prairies from Regina to Fort Macleod. There was ugly talk of lynching. Though there was some suspicion by police that the murderers of Peter Smith and Samuel Poole might have been white men, the populace mostly blamed the Indians and half-breeds. Their suspicions were strengthened when the killers of McLeish were identified as half-breeds James Gaddy, a notorious horse thief with a prison record, and Moise Racette. Captured in the United States that winter, they were executed at Regina in June 1888.

Despite the frenzied search, the summer passed with no arrests in the murder cases and no sign of The Dog and Big Rib. Then on the night of September 11, Sergeant Williams was on patrol with three constables from Fort Macleod when their attention was attracted by a campfire. A discreet investigation revealed that it was a small Indian camp some distance from the nearest reservation. Williams and his men silently surrounded the camp.

As Sergeant Williams stepped into the camp, the surprised Indians jumped up. Williams instantly recognized one as the fugitive Big Rib and, shouting a warning to his men, made a dive for him. In the following few minutes the camp was a scene of tumbling bodies. When the dust settled and the police had sorted themselves out, they discovered that Big Rib and the others had decamped. Their sole trophy was a Blood Indian named Eagle Rib who was escorted to Fort Macleod where he received three months for obstruction.

Two weeks later, The Dog ventured into Fort Macleod and wandered around the streets until he was recognized by one of the town patrol. The policeman seized him but simultaneously three Indians leaped into the fray. In the melee The Dog broke loose and ran for his pony. A mounted patrol galloped after the whooping warrior, but his lead was too great. After firing several shots at him the patrol returned to the barracks.

From time to time The Dog and Big Rib were sighted, but always they managed to keep a respectful distance from police patrols. For the next seventeen months the cat-and-mouse game continued, but the two outlaws seemed to be losing their zest for the chase. The relationship between the Indians and the police had been steadily improving and the cause of the outlaws seemed less important to the other braves. Consequently, when Sergeant Hilliard attended the Sun Dance on the Blood Reserve at Standoff in March 1890 and spotted The Dog among the spectators, he was able to effect an arrest with little difficulty. Two days later, Big Rib came voluntarily into the police post and surrendered. He was accompanied by another Blood Indian, Sharp Eyes, who had also taken part in the theft of Watson's horses three years before.

Judge McLeod sentenced Sharp Eyes to one year's detention at Lethbridge, while re-imposing the five-year sentences on The Dog and Big Rib. This time they made all the train connections to Stony Mountain Penitentiary. Ironically, they were both pardoned within a year. They were fortunate that they committed their thieving on the Canadian side of the border. As noted in the preceding article on Jingling Bells, across the border in Dakota or Montana irate ranchers would undoubtedly have "telegraphed them home."

Phantoms of the Rangeland

They were worth $3,000 dead or alive. Yet for eighteen months the two killers led police on an empty chase through thousands of square miles of British Columbia's cattle country.

The Cariboo region of British Columbia covers a sprawling plateau-like area some 320 km (200 miles) long from Ashcroft in the south to Quesnel in the north, and from the silt-laden waters of the Fraser River on the west to the glacier-clad Cariboo Mountains on the east. First settled by white men during the 1860s when the Cariboo Mountains yielded over $100 million in gold, it evolved into ranching country with thousands of whitefaced Herefords roaming its bunchgrass valleys and timbered sidehills. But for eighteen months beginning in 1911 more than cattle

Paul Spintlum, opposite page, and Moses Paul and freight teams on the Cariboo Wagon Road. The rangeland chase started with the murder of a teamster.

were at home on the Cariboo rangeland. During this period two killers, Indians Paul Spintlum and Moses Paul, skilfully used the rugged gullies and tree-clad ridges to elude the men who sought to bring them to justice for the murder of three men.

The story began on a hot mid-July day in 1911 when a Cariboo freight team driver, Louis Crosina, ran into the police office in the hamlet of Clinton and excitedly announced to Constable Jack McMillan that he had seen a dead man in Suicide Valley.

"How do you know he's dead?" asked McMillan.

"He's not only dead," said Crosina. "He's been murdered. His head's bashed in."

Promptly McMillan rode with Crosina some four miles south down the Cariboo wagon road to the valley appropriately named since it had been the scene of three suicides. Here he found the remains of a teamster called William Whyte. Just as Crosina had said, it looked like murder. Nearby was a blood-stained rock which matched the injuries at the back of Whyte's skull.

The body lay some distance from the road, partly concealed by a log, and could only have been seen by someone riding on a wagon. From its condition, the corpse had been lying there about three days. After searching for further clues, McMillan arranged for the removal of the body to Clinton.

In the course of subsequent enquiries McMillan learned from the Clinton postmaster that Whyte had been driving a team for Billy Parker at Big Lake. When he was laid off, he had been waiting in Clinton for his wages due to arrive by the first stagecoach. "His letter didn't come," said the postmaster, "and he seemed pretty disappointed."

McMillan learned more by chance from Chew Wye, a Chinese wood-chopper who lived in a cabin near Four Mile Lake. A week before, Chew told McMillan, Whyte had stopped in for a moment. He was a little drunk, and had a bottle of whiskey in his pocket. As he was leaving, from a nearby bush came an Indian on horseback. Whyte gave him a drink, then climbed up behind him and the pair rode off.

"Did you know the Indian?" asked McMillan.

"Sure," said Chew. "It was Moses Paul."

McMillan knew Paul, a rangy twenty-five-year-old who had never been in trouble with the law. In fact, he had taught McMillan's young daughter, Sadie, how to ride. McMillan was reluctant to accept the possibility that Paul had anything to do with Whyte's death. Nevertheless, he paid Moses Paul a visit and was surprised to find him singularly reticent. He merely stated that after a couple of drinks he and Whyte had parted a few miles from Chew's cabin. However, while searching Paul's cabin, McMillan found a watch in the loft.

The discovery of the watch convinced McMillan that Moses Paul might have been involved in Whyte's murder. He took Paul to Clinton's jail — a building that had seen little use since the last murder had been committed twenty years before — and continued his investigations.

A few days later, while McMillan was getting in some hay, Paul escaped.

McMillan soon learned that Paul Spintlum, a friend of Moses Paul, had recently purchased a stock of groceries and rifle ammunition at Bob Fraser's store. Could he be the one who helped Moses Paul escape? If so, McMillan now had two men to chase, both Chilcotin Indians who knew the country like a book, were adept at covering their tracks, and probably able to get help from friends and relatives. Furthermore, he strongly suspected that Moses Paul had murdered William Whyte since the watch he found in Paul's loft had been identified as belonging to the dead teamster.

A few weeks later, McMillan's suspicions were confirmed when Ah Joe, a friend of woodcutter Chew Wye, called at Chew's cabin. There was no sign of life, no wisp of smoke from the tin smoke stack. Pushing open the door, Ah Joe was shocked to see his friend lying on the floor, his head covered in blood. A blood stained axe lay beside him.

Ah Joe trotted the four miles into Clinton to tell his incoherent story to Constable McMillan. Surveying the cabin shortly afterwards, McMillan felt sure the killer was someone known to Wye to be able to hit him from behind with his own axe. Outside, McMillan found tracks of two men who had stood on a small knoll overlooking the cabin, probably waiting for Chew Wye's return. They had to be Paul and Spintlum — one of them getting rid of the witness to Paul's association with the murdered Whyte.

McMillan wired details to Chief Constable Joe Burr some twenty miles away at Ashcroft. Burr arrived on the next stagecoach with three constables. After the inquest with the verdict of "murdered by person or persons unknown," the search for the fugitives continued.

Like will-o'-the-wisps, they were reported here, then there, then somewhere else, only to vanish before the police arrived. After weeks of relentless searching the police realized that their biggest handicap was the aid given the two Indians by fellow tribesmen. They were not only being supplied with food, shelter and fresh horses, but also with the movements of their pursuers.

The best chance for the police was to keep the pair on the run and hope for a lucky break. But months passed with no sign of the men. McMillan had now been superseded by Constable Lee who, after a few months, resigned from the force. His place was taken by a young Scot, Constable Alec Kindness. When the Spring Assizes opened in Clinton on May 3, 1912, nearly a year had passed since Whyte's murder. The police had not even seen the wanted pair, let alone arrested them.

The Assizes were always an event of great interest in small communities. Clinton was no different and that morning as a group of townsmen smoked and gossiped outside the courthouse, their attention was suddenly drawn to a lone horseman galloping into town. His arrival signalled the break the police had been waiting for.

The rider was Charlie Truran, a homesteader employed at nearby Pollard's Ranch who that morning had been searching for a couple of strayed horses. After crossing Mile 51 Creek he had spotted a pair of horses downstream under some trees. As he rode up close, two men leaped from the underbrush, each grabbing a rifle.

It was then, Truran said, that he realized he was looking at Paul and

Spintlum. The Indians eyed him stonily, and Truran pretended not to recognize them.

"I lost a couple of horses. You fellows seen them?"

Truran's question was met with stolid indifference.

"If you see them," he said, "let me know and I'll give you $10." It was a handsome offer since the going rate for returning a strayed horse was $2.50.

"Okay," said one of the outlaws with a smirk. "If we find them, we'll let you know."

Truran turned his horse and, not without a sense of fear, slowly walked away. Once out of sight he applied his spurs and galloped into Clinton.

On hearing the story Constable Kindness at once formed a posse consisting of Jimmy Boyd and Bill Ritchie of Clinton, Constable Forest Loring, an Assize witness from Ashcroft, and George Carson of Pavilion. Armed with Winchesters they galloped to Pollard's Ranch were Charlie Pollard joined them. At this point, Truran's enthusiasm for the chase waned and his place was taken by Johnny, the rancher's son.

When the riders reached the trees where Truran had met the outlaws, a quick look round showed the direction in which they had gone. Pressing on at full gallop, the posse soon overtook a packhorse, its lead rope dragging.

"Come on boys, we're crowding 'em," yelled Boyd. "They've had to drop that horse."

Constable W. Fernie and his Indian trackers trailed the two outlaws for weeks.

Then leaning over to Kindness, he suggested the constable drop to the rear. "I know these fellows," he said. "They won't hurt me, but you're a policeman. They'll shoot you sure as hell."

Kindness grinned acknowledgment but retained his lead position. The consequence would be tragic.

Almost before the horsemen knew it, they rounded a bend in the trail and came to a hoof-stamping halt in front of some windfallen trees. A rifle cracked from behind the fallen timber. Kindness slumped forward in his saddle, then slid to the ground — dead.

Two more shots rang out as the posse milled around in confusion. Loring felt a hammer-blow to his wrist as a bullet broke it. Boyd dismounted, and pumped shot after shot at the outlaw's hideout. Loring, clasping his wrist, moved out of range, while Ritchie risked the fusilade to pull Kindness' body to shelter.

Ritchie said later that when he realized Kindness was dead, he looked up in time to see Boyd, who had run out of ammunition, bravely charging toward the outlaws. He was ready to use his gun as a club. Fortunately, the Indians had vanished.

With the murder of Constable Kindness, the police realized they were dealing with cold-blooded killers. The head of the B.C. Provincial Police force, Superintendent Colin S. Campbell, arrived at Clinton and immediately wired to Kamloops for Chief Constable W.L. Fernie to join him. Fernie brought with him Alphonse Ignace, a Shuswap Indian known for his tracking ability, and six helpers. Fernie was to state later: "For skill in tracking, I'd place those Shuswaps with the world's best — including the Australian blacks."

About three weeks after the death of Kindness, Al Neas, a rancher at Big Bar Creek northwest of Clinton, rode over to fellow rancher Bill Janes at Desolation Ranch to get a horse. Although they were only 29 km (18 miles) from Clinton, neither had heard about the policeman's murder. Neas stayed overnight with his friend and in the morning went out to the barn to find that his saddle was missing. He asked if Janes had moved it.

"Never touched it," was his friend's response.

The pair returned to the barn to have another look. The saddle peg was near an open window and as they conjectured where the saddle might have gone, they heard a movement in the yard. It was Fernie and his trackers.

It was then the pair heard the story of the Clinton killing and how Fernie and his men had trailed the Indians for twenty-one days. One of the outlaws, they reported, was mounted, the other on foot. Sometimes one ran beside the horse, occasionally both were mounted. As the tracks led to the barn it was obvious they had taken the saddle.

From Desolation Ranch the tracks led into the turfy Big Bar Lake country. From there the trail turned north, then west, and alternated across high ridges so that the fugitives could scan the back country with field glasses stolen from another rancher. It led into the Rafael Lake country, then back to Big Bar and later, from a ridge, down toward the Fraser River and the Canoe Creek Indian Reserve. At the Reserve, Fernie's questions brought evasive answers or obstinate silence.

The trail now led into boulder-strewn country. Here, on one occasion, Fernie began to doubt the reliability of his Indian helpers. Even though Alphonse was uncannily clever in reading trail signs, Fernie finally suggested that he may have lost the trail. Alphonse gave a fleeting smile and cantered down a dry creek bed into a patch of cottonwoods. He pointed to hoof marks then, scanning the shoulder high willows nearby, singled out a leaf for Fernie's inspection. One leaf. But it bore a faint black smudge from being rubbed by a fire-blackened cooking pot slung on a saddle.

The next day, the trackers came so suddenly on the outlaws' camp that the fire was still burning briskly. That Paul and Spintlum had fled in great haste was proved by the flour, rice and sugar they left behind. Fernie and his men spurred after them but soon were baffled by a confusion of horse tracks on the trail.

"They herd wild horses ahead of them to cover tracks. Old Indian trick," explained the sagacious Alphonse. It took the best part of a day to pick up the trail and then it led toward the Bonaparte River.

Near Fish Lake, 160 km (100 miles) south of Canoe Creek Reserve, the pursuers discovered that they were not far behind their quarry. They found an abandoned horse which had been stolen, then learned of another one stolen to replace it. Fernie estimated that he was only some fourteen hours behind the pair — but he was worried. If the outlaws reached the vast mountainous Clearwater country to the northeast the chase could go on for years.

As weeks passed the Indians were reported in Empire Valley, then at Big Fish Lake were Fernie thought he saw a movement on an island in the lake. There was a little scow-type boat nearby so he and Alphonse paddled over to the island. There had been movement, true enough, but it was caused by the island's only inhabitant — a buck deer.

Toward the end of summer came a report that the outlaws had been seen at Porcupine Creek above Kelly Lake in the southern Cariboo. An Indian tracker, Cultus Jack, trailed them to Jimmy Wood's place then lost the trail high up on a stony ridge. They'd been there all right but had vanished like smoke.

A week later Bill Pearson of the Kelly Lake Ranch reported seeing two saddled horses standing near the lake, and figured the wanted men had jumped into the bush to escape notice. Old Strawnick, Moses Paul's mother, was friendly with the Pearsons and pleaded with Mrs. Pearson not to let her son join the chase.

"He be killed for sure," she warned, adding that on the day Paul broke jail she had put a curse on the police.

Curse or no curse, the chase went on until it became clear that the outlaws had either crossed the Fraser and gone into the Camelsfoot Mountains, or crossed Kelly Lake into the Hat Creek country. Two constables searched without results but they did learn that the Nicola Indians would have nothing to do with the killers. This rejection might mean that the outlaws had been forced into the hills near Hat Creek.

By now it was fall, and snow would soon shroud the Cariboo. The police decided on a fresh approach. They had scoured thousands of square miles of undulating rangeland, crossed scores of creeks and spent months on the trail. While they had come tantalizingly close to the murderers, they had yet to see either one, although the incredible skill shown by the Indian trackers in following the circuitous indistinct trail became a legend in the cattle country.

On November 15, Chief Constable Burr spoke with several Indian Chiefs, pointing out that support of law and order was both white men's and Indians' business. If they wanted future support from the law then their people would have to stop assisting those who had so callously murdered three men. The Chiefs seemed to see the wisdom in this statement and asked for a month in which to talk it over with their people.

Word soon drifed in to Clinton that a lot of parlaying was going on among the Indians. The talks appeared to be bringing a favorable result for indications were that the outlaws were going to be handed over.

On December 15, 1912, Burr got in touch with Thomas Cummiski, then Superintendent of Indian Agencies for British Columbia. He asked to hold a meeting with the Chiefs and get their collective answer, pointing out that the month had gone by and it was time for action. He also suggested that if the Chiefs did not co-operate, they should be deposed and new ones appointed.

Cummiski agreed and subsequently reported that he had arranged a meeting near Ashcroft where the outlaws would be handed over. But there were conditions. The killers were not to be handcuffed. They were to be provided with legal counsel. In addition, medals were to be presented to the Chiefs who had engineered the surrender as an indication of their support for law and order.

In the late afternoon of December 30, Superintendent Cummiski in company with six picked Chiefs went to the Bonaparte Reserve near Ashcroft. With no police present and with little ceremony, Paul and Spintlum were handed over to Cummiski. The long, eighteen-month rangeland pursuit had ended without further loss of life.

There was a standing reward of $3,000 for the capture of the murderers, and the B.C. government thought it was a good idea to split the money among the Chiefs. They refused. "There's blood on it," was their opinion.

In accordance with the agreement, the government had six impressive medals made, each inscribed with a Chief's name and brief details of how he earned it. When presentation day came, however, the Chiefs refused them. The medals, still brightly new, are today in the Provincial Archives in Victoria.

The prisoners were escorted to Kamloops Jail, both showing obvious signs of the hardships they had undergone. After two trials — one at Vernon, the other at New Westminster — Moses Paul was found guilty of murder and Spintlum adjudged an accessory after the fact. Paul was hanged at Kamloops Jail on December 12, 1913, while Spintlum, suffering from tuberculosis, died soon after starting a life sentence. Thus closed the saga of the longest manhunt in the history of the Cariboo. It was a hunt that justified Constable Fernie's faith in his Indian trackers — the men he placed "with the world's best."

Alberta's Frontier Detective

The policeman disobeyed orders to destroy the muskrat cap. Incredibly, it would then help send an Alberta murderer to the gallows.

Detective Sergeant J. D. Nicholson.

One of the most remarkable cases in the frontier history of Western Canada was the relentless pursuit of William Oscar King by Detective Sergeant J.D. Nicholson of the Royal North-West Mounted Police. The trail led from Millet, Alberta, to Bemidji, Minnesota; from witness to witness; from suspicion to certainty; and involved pure chance, intelligence, cunning and determination on both sides of the contest.

The saga began on the afternoon of March 10, 1907, when a sleigh containing two men was seen proceeding in a southerly direction near Millet, Alberta. Normally a sleigh on a lonely winter road attracts no more than passing attention, but there were several unusual features about this incident that remained in the memory of those who saw it. The trail was not yet opened and was a difficult one to travel, leading only to the homestead of James Aecker a few miles to the west. The team that drew the sleigh was unusual, consisting of a magnificent big black horse with a

The case started with the murder of Joseph A. Hindahl near the Alberta community of Millet.

William Oscar King.

heavy neck and a smaller, almost insignificant bay mare. Finally, the same sleigh was seen returning over the trail an hour and a half later, but this time there was only one man on the high spring seat.

Later that afternoon, James Aecker passed along the trail and noticed what appeared to be a dead muskrat lying beside the road. He thought nothing of it but when he came upon a trail of blood farther along the road, he turned back to re-examine the "muskrat." It proved to be a grey muskrat cap. There was a cut in the cloth of the crown and the cap was caked with frozen blood.

On his arrival at Wetaskiwin, Aecker handed the cap to Staff Sergeant Charles Phillips of the RNWMP, who immediately returned with the settler to where the cap had been found. He ascertained that a team and two men had camped on the little-frequented trail, had made dinner and started out again in a westward direction. A short distance from the temporary camp, the sleigh had made an about turn and retraced its tracks. It was here that Aecker had discovered the cap. Most significant was the trail of frozen blood between the marks of the sleigh runners.

It was not difficult to trace the progress of the sleigh with its single remaining passenger, but it was time consuming. Not until late the following afternoon was Phillips able to track it to Leduc where a check at the Waldorf Hotel revealed that a man signing himself "A. Schmidt" had taken his sleigh to the livery stable, stayed the night and left early that morning. When questioned, the livery man stated that Schmidt had been careful of the contents of the sleigh, parking it in the darkest corner of the yard. However, he had noticed that it contained farm equipment.

Following the trail northward, Staff Sergeant Phillips traced the team to Edmonton and a house on Fraser Flats. But here the trail ended. He questioned Oscar Koenig who answered the general description of the man who had rented the room at Leduc, but nothing came of this interview. Returning to his post, Phillips wrote a report and sent it and the blood-stained cap to headquarters in Edmonton.

The cap and report lay for weeks at the Mounted Police barracks in Edmonton. Summer came and so did complaints that the cap was beginning to smell unpleasant. Since nothing had come to light regarding its owner, nor had a missing person been reported who might conceivably have worn it, the commanding officer ordered it destroyed. However, the constable to whom the order was given disobeyed. Whether prompted by some instinct not to destroy possible evidence, or feeling exuberant about his forthcoming discharge from the force, he placed the malodorous cap on a beam in the cellar of the barracks and shortly took his discharge and went to work in Edmonton.

Over a year later in September 1908, William Oscar King, a prisoner detained in the Edmonton police barracks, sent for Detective Sergeant J.D. Nicholson. Nicholson was engaged on a case of fraud and horse stealing against King and his two confederates, Gus Borden and August Tyman, who were still at large. Hoping for a confession, or lead to the whereabouts of Borden and Tyman, Nicholson went to the cells. He was not prepared for the story King unfolded.

King, alias Koenig, alias Keller, alias Schultz, had been born in

Saxony, Germany, in 1872. After immigrating to the United States, where he became a naturalized citizen, he entered Canada in 1901 and drifted to the Edmonton district shortly after the formation of the province of Alberta in 1905. A remarkable rascal, he had teamed up with several others — among them Tyman and Borden— who spent their time between mining jobs padding their pocketbooks with assorted thefts, frauds and shady horse deals. Never underestimating this man, Detective Nicholson conducted his questioning warily.

King wanted to make a deal. In return for a lighter sentence, he promised to reveal some interesting information about Gus Borden. Without committing himself, Nicholson obtained from King the startling information that sometime during the spring of 1907, Borden had murdered a man near Clover Bar Bridge, some 15 km (9 miles) east of Edmonton. He had learned of the murder from August Tyman. The body was buried in a manure pile at an old construction camp, which had burned to the ground in the summer of 1908, a short distance from the bridge. King was confident that he could locate the spot.

The following morning, Detective Sergeant Nicholson drove to Clover Bar with King and a party of police. After some searching, King located the manure pile and within a few minutes the police had unearthed the remains of what had once been a human being. Further searching produced a stained pen knife and part of a woollen sweater.

From the condition of the sweater and bones, it was obvious that an effort had been made to burn them before concealing them in the manure heap. King could not supply the name of the victim, nor was anything discovered which threw light on his identity. With only charred bones to go by, there was not even the certainty that murder had been committed. The party returned to Edmonton and the remains were turned over to Dr. Ravell, provincial pathologist at the University of Edmonton.

On the return trip to Edmonton, King gave Nicholson a further shock. This was but one of Borden's victims, the prisoner claimed. A second victim had been killed and his body buried in brush in the country west of Innisfail. King was also certain that he could pinpoint the location of this second body.

Nicholson escorted King to Innisfail on October 1, 1908, where they were joined by Corporal Rodgers of the local detachment. They then proceeded towards Markerville, some 40 km (25 miles) to the west. King, who up to this time had been smiling, confident and co-operative, now showed signs of hesitation. Several piles of brush, cleared from the land by homesteaders, were examined but none yielded a body.

Nicholson, who had been suspicious of the existence of this second body, was aware that King might be trying to make an escape. The reason for his choosing this desolate region could also mean that Borden or Tyman, or both, were in the vicinity.

After consulting with Corporal Rodgers, who knew the district intimately, the two policemen decided that if the wanted men were in the area they would probably be found at Ploughmacher's farm, three miles west of Markerville. Ploughmacher's reputation was not too savory and he was not above hiding fugitives if their pockets were lined. Shifting their

The muskrat hat worn by Joseph Hindahl the day he was murdered, the cuts left by the murder weapon near top left. Although the blood-stained cap was the only clue in the snow at the murder scene, it sent William Oscar King to the gallows. Edmonton in 1904. King burned Hindahl's body nearby at an abandoned construction site at Clover Bar Bridge.

attention from dead bodies to live ones, the police escorted their prisoner to the Ploughmacher farm.

The Ploughmacher place consisted of a house, a barn and a shack located on the edge of some bluffs. Selecting the shack as the most probable hiding place for a fugitive, the policemen drove their sleigh between the stable and the shack so that Rodgers could keep both under scrutiny while Nicholson checked the house. As it was approaching suppertime, Rodgers followed the custom of the country and began un-hitching the horses.

At the house, Nicholson discovered Mrs. Ploughmacher and a Mrs. Shultz, but no men. Neither of the women knew, or would reveal, anything about the wanted men.

While Rodgers was unhitching the team, he instructed King to take the first horse into the barn, so that he could keep watch on the shack. King obliged. He was too obliging. There was a momentary lapse of vigilance on the part of the Corporal and the wily King used it to slip out the rear of the stable and make his way into the bush.

Rodgers gave the alarm when King did not return from the stable for the second horse, but the delay was costly. Though both policemen started in pursuit and once caught sight of their quarry and fired a shot at him, King eluded them in the gathering dusk.

Fate, which was already preserving a mouldering fur cap on a ledge in the basement of the Mounted Police barracks in Edmonton, seemed determined that the duel between the wily King and Nicholson should be played out to the end. While police forces across the prairies were alerted to be on the watch for the fugitive, no one held too high a hope for his capture. Hunting a fugitive in this huge country, still sparsely settled, was like looking for a solitary flea on the hide of a Labrador. Nicholson, however, was a determined man.

While visiting a farm in the Innisfail district some time later on an entirely different matter, Nicholson noticed a photograph of King, taken with a woman and two children. He learned that the woman was King's wife and that the photograph had been taken in 1906 when the Kings had homesteaded in the district. Until then Nicholson had not known about King's wife, or that he had farmed in the area, but it helped to explain King's eagerness to return to the district when he made his escape. Taking the photograph back to Edmonton, Nicholson showed it to the wife of another of King's associates. She immediately recognized the woman in the picture and told the policeman that Mrs. King had left her husband and was living with a James Parks.

Allowing for the possibility that King, resenting his wife's desertion, might try to find her, Nicholson visited Mrs. King and warned her of this danger. She promised to co-operate with the police, but Nicholson sensed her co-operation stemmed primarily from fear rather than a desire to assist the police.

On the afternoon of April 23, 1909, Mrs. King discovered her estranged husband watching the Parks' house. She recognized him in spite of the beard he had grown. She was able to get a message to the Edmonton Police, who arrested King then turned him over to the welcoming arms of the RNWMP. To the original charge of fraud and horse theft was now added a charge of escaping from custody.

Fate now played its master stroke.

Sergeant Charles Phillips, of the Wetaskiwin detachment, chanced to visit headquarters during the period that King was being held. He saw King and recognized him as the man he had questioned about the blood-stained grey muskrat cap which had been found near Millet in March 1907. He thought nothing of the matter, but later in the day while talking to Nicholson, he mentioned the earlier incident.

Nicholson immediately saw a possible connection between the unknown man found at Clover Bar and the blood-stained cap. With a vigor that startled the visiting policeman, Nicholson began to shoot questions at him. Where was the hat?

Phillips recalled that he had sent it to headquarters with the customary report. Nicholson took it from there, but soon ran into a stone wall. The Commanding Officer recalled having ordered it destroyed, and assumed that his order had been carried out. Nicholson now displayed the exceptional qualities of an investigative ability that was to make him one of the great frontier detectives. Not content with a blank wall, he learned the name of the man to whom the order had been given, tracked him to his place of employment and was rewarded with the happy information that — for once — a Mountie had disobeyed orders. The cap was unearthed from its resting place and turned over to Dr. Ravell, the pathologist who was still trying to piece together the bone fragments found at Clover Bar.

At Wetaskiwin a muskrat cap worn by the murdered man started a series of events that sent the killer to the gallows.

In June 1909, William Oscar King was sentenced to seven years in the newly opened penitentiary at Edmonton on four charges of fraud, two of horse stealing and one of escape. With his quarry secured for a lengthy period, Nicholson started weaving the chain of circumstantial evidence of a much more serious crime.

Returning to Mrs. King, he began a campaign of winning her confidence. Certain from his initial visit that she was unwilling to co-operate because of her basic suspicious nature, he now saw that her reticence stemmed from a much deeper motive. Gradually, by reassurance and patience, he got her story and the reason for her reluctance to speak out.

She first met King in Germany in 1895. A child was born and when a second child was imminent they had married. They immigrated to the United States and from there to Montreal and finally to Alberta. Here King, after trying to homestead in the Innisfail district, had given up and taken a job at the mine at Clover Bar.

In November 1906, Joseph Hindahl, their Innisfail neighbor and an immigrant from Bemidji, Minnesota, had come to live with them at Clover Bar. He, too, worked at the mine. She described him as a sober, respectable man, between 40 and 50, of medium height, and bow-legged. He had jet black hair and wore a mustache, but the most notable characteristic was his voice which was coarse and deep.

In early March 1907, both men left Clover Bar in Hindahl's sleigh, planning to ready Hindahl's homestead for the spring. A few days later

King returned alone with Hindahl's team and equipment. He told his wife that their friend had caught cold on the trip, died and was buried on the homestead. But when she discovered her husband burning some of Hindahl's clothing, and later when he disposed of the horses and rig, she was certain that something was wrong.

After Mrs. King related her story, she accompanied Nicholson to the site of the burned construction camp where the Kings had lived. However, the fall growth of weeds around the location made a search impossible.

For some months, Nicholson was occupied with other tasks, but the case of the muskrat cap and remains of the unknown man still occupied his spare moments. Meanwhile, pathologist Dr. Ravell had fitted together the charred skull bones of the Clover Bar corpse. From the structure of the jawbone, Dr. Ravell was able to determine that its owner had a receding chin, and from the remainder of the bones, he estimated that they were of a man of slender build and medium height, who had been somewhat bow-legged. The pathologist's findings tallied with Mrs. King's description of Hindahl.

A number of coarse black hairs had been found inside the muskrat cap and might have been similar to those of the dead man. Of more importance, when the cut in the cap was compared to a cut in the skull, it matched perfectly.

Nicholson now was certain that he had probably met death on the lonely trail west of Millet. To prove that William King had murdered him was a different matter since a major problem was establishing how Hindahl's body had been taken from the death scene to Clover Bar.

In the spring of 1910, when winter's decay had levelled the weeds and warm weather had not yet spawned a new crop, Nicholson and Mrs. King returned to Clover Bar. He found the remains of a fire where Mrs. King indicated and, sifting it carefully, retrieved part of a red woollen blanket and remnants of a suit. Mrs. King unhesitatingly identified them as part of Hindahl's equipment. Shown the fur cap, she said that she had seen him with one just like it.

Assured no doubt by the fact that her husband was safely incarcerated, Mrs. King overcame her natural instinct for self-protection and began to involve herself, King and her present spouse — James Parks. After Hindahl's disappearance, she said, King had gone to Minnesota and returned with nearly $300. He had given her Hindahl's bankbook for safe-keeping and entrusted a watch to Parks.

When produced, the bankbook showed a considerable sum on credit to Joseph A. Hindahl at the Hennypinn State Bank at Minneapolis. Nicholson impounded the bankbook. The watch given to Parks had been sold to a Canadian National Railway conductor who later sold it to a bartender at the Queen's Hotel in Edmonton. Nicholson located the bartender, who still had the watch, and bought it back for $15 — the sum he had given the conductor.

Certain now that a strong chain of circumstantial evidence was being forged against King, Nicholson went to Hindahl's homestead and questioned his neighbors, showing them the watch, the penknife and the photograph. At the farm of Swan Borg, he struck a gold mine of information. Borg, a close friend of the dead man, identified the watch and penknife. His wife, who had once tried to scratch Hindahl's initials on the back of the watch with a darning needle, pointed out the scratches.

Methodically, Nicholson went over the previous investigation made by Sergeant Phillips. Armed with the photograph and a description of the horse team, he questioned the livery stable owner and found that he remembered the oddly matched team. He also recalled that there had been an oblong shape in the sleigh, wrapped in canvas. The clerk at the Waldorf Hotel identified King's photograph as a likeness of the man who had registered on March 10, thus confirming that William Oscar King and A. Schmidt were the same.

Back in Edmonton, Nicholson traced the team to the local auction mart. The auctioneer identified King's picture as that of the man who gave him the horses to sell. Better still, he remembered the man who purchased them. This person was contacted. He still had the horses and was ready to testify when called upon.

Nicholson, carrying the photograph, bank book, watch and knife, journeyed to Minneapolis where a bank teller at the Hennypin State Bank identified King from the photo. The teller said King had presented the bank book in late March 1907 and tried to withdraw $400. When asked for identification, the man left the bank without the money and did not return.

At Hindahl's hometown of Bemidji, Nicholson interviewed the murdered man's neighbors who identified the penknife and watch, and described the wagon and team perfectly. T.J. Miller, a money lender, recognized King and said that on June 19, 1907, King, forging Hindahl's signature, had applied for a loan against his Bemidji farm property. King returned two days later to complete the loan and again signed Hindahl's name to a receipt for $264.75.

Positive now that he had enough evidence to lay a charge of murder against King, Nicholson returned to Edmonton. The trial opened on June 6, 1910.

Mr. Justice Scott was on the bench. Prosecutor E.B. Cogswell and his assistant, the renowned Patrick Nolan, presented thirty-two witnesses to the six-man jury. For the defence, Harry H. Robertson, already famous for his adept cross-examinations, strove hard to loosen the rope steadily tightening around his client's neck. Through five days of unseasonable heat the jury listened to evidence. In the end they were convinced by Dr. Ravell's skilful testimony that the body found at Clover Bar was that of Hindahl, and that he had come to his death at the hands of the prisoner on the lonely trail west of Millett. After two hours, they rendered their verdict of guilty and heard the judge pronounce the death sentence.

King was hanged, still maintaining his innocence, at 7:30 a.m., August 2, 1910.

Nearly two years before King himself had involved Detective Sergeant J.D. Nicholson when he tried to blame his some-time companions, Borden and Tyman, for the murder. Ironically, the more the persistent Nicholson followed the evidence, the more inexorably King was drawn to the gallows.

He was a devout churchman, totally
respected by his neighbors. Yet one morning he
kissed his wife goodbye and drove off to
singlehandedly pull

Saskatchewan's First Stagecoach Holdup

On the morning of July 12, 1886, George L. Garnett, ferryman for the
South Branch crossing of the Saskatchewan River, hitched up his bay
mare. Then he kissed his wife goodbye, gave last-minute instructions to
the relief ferryman he had hired and drove off into the pages of history.
He was about to undertake Saskatchewan's first and only stagecoach
holdup.

Four days later, Garnett showed up at Salt Springs, some 65 km (40
miles) south of Humboldt on the Qu'Appelle-Prince Albert Trail. Salt
Springs was an important way station for the mail drivers since the southbound stage from Prince Albert met and exchanged passengers and mail
with the north-bound coaches from the CPR mainline at Qu'Appelle. At 7
o'clock on the evening of July 16, both stages arrived on schedule and laid
over for the night. Shortly after their arrival, Garnett rode north out of
town.

He was up with the sun and left after a hasty breakfast. From time to
time he stopped on a hill to survey the back trail, but there was no sign of
the north-bound. Then a few kilometers north of Salt Springs, he came
upon five men asleep in their camp beside the trail.

There had been nothing in the career of George L. Garnett to account

for what he did next. Born in London, Ontario, he had come West during the 1885 Riel Rebellion. After serving with the 7th Fusiliers, he settled in Winnipeg, where he married and then moved to South Branch to run the ferry. Well respected by his neighbors and a devout churchman, he had added to his esteem by operating the ferry efficiently — a rarity in those days. He was to prove an equally efficient holdup man, beginning with the sleeping five men.

When there was no response to his summons, Garnett fired two shots into the air. Almost at once the sleepy men, still suffering the effects of too much whiskey the night before, tumbled into the morning sunlight. They blinked in surprise at the unmasked bandit. Pretending to have a partner concealed nearby, Garnett relieved them of their wallets and loose change, close to $300, then left.

Towards 1 p.m., about 40 km (23 miles) south of Humboldt, Garnett stopped the Prince Albert stage. It was driven by John Art and carried two passengers — Edward Fiddler, a farmer from Prince Albert, and John Betts, a prominent politician. Still scorning a mask, Garnett waved a double-barrelled shotgun at the surprised trio and ordered them from the stage. When they hesitated to obey, he cocked the shotgun. They jumped.

At top is the Battleford-Edmonton stagecoach in front of a sod-roofed cabin in the late 1880s. Below is Prince Albert where Garnett was recognized and arrested.

Garnett forced Art and Betts to kneel while he trussed their arms, and under threat of the gun made Fiddler conceal the stage behind a bluff. Safely off the road, Garnett lost little time. "Driver, where is the box?"

"I don't know nothing about a box," John Art replied.

Garnett leaped onto the stage but failed to locate a strong-box. He kicked the mail sacks to the ground, ripped them open and selected the registered letters. John Art shifted his feet in embarrassment. "I feel awful silly letting one man hold us up," he protested.

"You needn't," Garnett assured him. "My partner and I held up a larger party than your's this morning. He's over there behind the bluff covering you now."

Although he searched the three men, he took nothing — not even Betts' $250 in cash. As a final gesture of goodwill, Garnett shared with them a bottle of whiskey he had found on the stage.

Garnett's concept of the way to commit a crime is one of the strangest on record. Having left behind eight men capable of identifying him, he rode back to Salt Springs. Here he retrieved his cart and then drove 160 km (100 miles) to Carrot River where he sought to establish an alibi by registering a homestead. That done, he returned to his ferry and, in the presence of his substitute ferryman, shaved off his distinctive beard and mustache.

The proceeds of the two robberies was $1,465.40. Aftering burying the money in a tin can a short distance from the ferry, Garnett resumed his duties and his accustomed role of respectability.

Garnett's ferry over the South Saskatchewan River and John F. Betts, one of the passengers on the stagecoach which Garnett held up.

A month later, business took Garnett to Prince Albert and there retribution overtook him. He was recognized by John Art, the stagecoach driver, and arrested by the North-West Mounted Police. A preliminary hearing was held before Superintendent Perry and Garnett was sent to Regina to stand trial.

Perry immediately issued a search warrant to locate the missing money. Though the police tore up Garnett's home, ripped planks from his ferry and prowled the surrounding brush, all they found were several articles of clothing later identified by the victims as those worn by Garnett.

While in Regina prison awaiting trial, Garnett disclosed the location of his cache to a cell-mate, Peter Smith, who operated a stagecoach stopping house near Touchwood. When Smith was released early in September he hired a half-breed guide and went straight to the cache. Elated with his new-found wealth, Smith gave the ferryman $5 for use of the ferry and another $5 for a meal. For Smith, however, the money proved fatal.

Apparently of a shrewder nature than Garnett, Smith returned to his shack beside the Prince Albert Trail. Police suspicion focused on him briefly but as he had outwardly resumed his meager way of life, interest in him soon waned. The following May, Smith announced his intention of leaving. When he did disappear, nobody thought much about it.

Some days later, Smith's body was found in the bushes by a passing freighter. Suspicion centered on an Indian boy, Nan-nan-kase-lex. He had suddenly acquired a unusual amount of money, and large sums of cash were not part of the way of life for either Indians or settlers in the 1880s. He was taken to Regina, charged with the murder of Peter Smith, and examined by Inspector Norman of the NWMP. Nan-nan-kase-lex said the money had been given to him by an Indian woman friend. While no supportive evidence was forthcoming, the investigation revealed the then unknown account of Smith's visit to the Garnett ferry for the hidden money.

Garnett's trial opened on October 7, 1886, before Judge Hugh Richardson. The evidence conclusively tied him to the crimes. Despite the testimony of three character witnesses — including Archdeacon Marsh, who had travelled from Winnipeg at considerable expense — Garnett was sentenced to fourteen years. While the sentence was severe in view of his past record of honesty and industry, Judge Richardson declared that a harsh penalty was necessary to discourage the lawless element from preying upon defenceless stagecoaches.

As Convict 23, Garnett settled into the bleak routine of Stony Mountain Penitentiary, near Winnipeg. Since he had always been closely associated with the church, it was no surprise when he obtained the position of servant to the chaplain. Two years later, however, there was a surprise — Garnett purloined a suit of clothes belonging to the preacher, walked out of the prison and rode away in the padre's horse and buggy.

As with his stagecoach holdup, Garnett's prison escape was notable for lack of careful planning. He was soon again safely on the inside. After serving eight years he was pardoned and vanished from the records of Western badmen.

The Saga of Simon Gun-an-Noot

In the mountain wilderness of Northwestern British Columbia this Kispiox Indian eluded police for thirteen years. When he finally surrendered he was found innocent of the murders which had put a $1,000 reward on him.

Simon Gun-an-Noot.

In Western Canada's past history, many a colorful character with a gun in his hand and a price on his head has taken to the wide open spaces. If his vivid career has ended on a slab or in a cell, for a brief time he is something of a celebrity. Of these fugitives, a bare handful have become a sort of legend. These few include men like Bill Miner (see Heritage House book, *Bill Miner . . . STAGECOACH & TRAIN ROBBER),* and that most famous of all Indian outlaws, Simon Gun-an-Noot. He is famous because after dodging police for an unbelievable thirteen years, he surrendered and was found innocent of the murder charge that originally made him an outlaw.

Simon was a Kispiox full blood, his home at Hagwilget close to

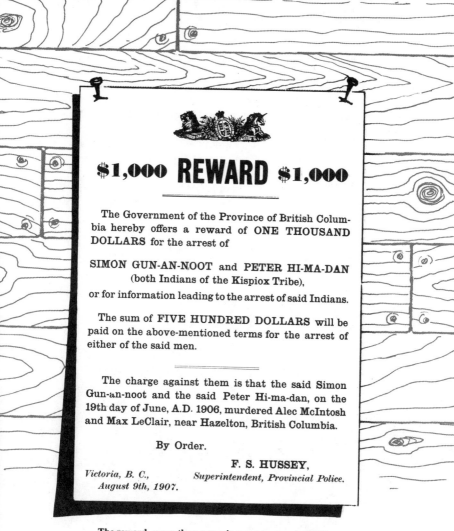

$1,000 **REWARD** $1,000

The Government of the Province of British Columbia hereby offers a reward of ONE THOUSAND DOLLARS for the arrest of

SIMON GUN-AN-NOOT and PETER HI-MA-DAN
(both Indians of the Kispiox Tribe),

or for information leading to the arrest of said Indians.

The sum of FIVE HUNDRED DOLLARS will be paid on the above-mentioned terms for the arrest of either of the said men.

The charge against them is that the said Simon Gun-an-noot and the said Peter Hi-ma-dan, on the 19th day of June, A.D. 1906, murdered Alec McIntosh and Max LeClair, near Hazelton, British Columbia.

By Order.

F. S. HUSSEY,
Superintendent, Provincial Police.

Victoria, B. C.,
August 9th, 1907.

The reward, more than a year's average wage in 1907.

Hazelton in the mountains of northwestern British Columbia. He was an impressive man, big for an Indian and not only proud and erect, but with muscles and sinews as tough as whipcord — the result of years of back-packing and canoeing. His very appearance hinted at his reputation as a successful hunter and trapper, and among whites he was known as a truthful and fair dealing man. He was converted to Christianity early in his youth, always proudly wearing his church medallion on feast days. As a husband Simon was devoted to his young wife, Sarah.

The saga of Gun-an-Noot began in June 1906 when he came out of the wilderness to sell his fur to the Hudson's Bay post at Hazelton. After squaring up his jawbone (credit) he left for home at Kispiox and that evening joined in a homecoming celebration at a nearby roadhouse at Two Mile.

While Simon wasn't exactly a drinking man, he did his share. Around midnight things got a bit noisy at the roadhouse and a miner called Alec McIntosh made some derogatory remarks about Indians in general, and the morality of Kispiox women in particular.

"Does that include my wife?" snapped Simon, as he seized a couple of fistfuls of McIntosh's shirt and pulled the miner within inches of his face.

"Yes, your wife, too!" sneered McIntosh in his half-drunken abandon. Simon's rock-hard fist cut off further comment and with McIntosh flat on the floor, he departed.

Around dawn the next day a party of Babine Indians walking the trail to Hagwilget found their path barred by a man sprawled on his back, dead. Hurrying to Hazelton they told Johnny Boyd of their discovery,

**The northwestern B.C. community
of Hazelton in 1912.**

who in turn passed on the information to Constable Jim Kirby of the Provincial Police. Shortly afterward, Kirby and the local coroner, Edward H. Hicks-Beach, were on the scene. The dead man was Alec McIntosh, his shirt front stained with blood, his face bruised and discolored, and the little finger of his right hand injured. When the body was turned over, reason for the blood on his chest was apparent. A bullet had caught him in the back and taken an upward course to exit just below his left collarbone. His horse was grazing nearby, and from tracks Kirby deduced that McIntosh had been galloping along the trail when someone stepped out of the bush behind him and shot either from a kneeling or a prone position.

Just as the constable and coroner were arranging for a wagon to take the dead man to Hazelton, a man named Gus Sampan came running up. There was, he said between excited breaths, another body on the trail about a mile and a half from Hazelton.

The second dead man was Max LeClair, also lying flat on his back.

He had been killed in the same fashion as McIntosh — hit in the back about two inches from his spine. Like McIntosh, LeClair had been riding, and again it appeared that someone had stepped out on the trail after he passed, knelt, and fired.

To Kirby and Hicks-Beach one thing was crystal clear: the man who did the shooting was certainly a marksman. But was it one man? How could he shoot one, then gallop to another vantage point to kill the other? Maybe there were two murderers? But then there was the coincidence of the bullet's point of impact. Rather uncanny!

In his enquiry Kirby interviewed those who had been at the party at Two Mile. Some were evasive, some reluctant, and some had such hangovers they didn't remember a thing. Out of it all, however, came some details of the altercation between McIntosh and Gun-an-Noot. Some were even prepared to swear they heard Gun-an-Noot threaten to kill Alec. There was also evidence that Peter Hi-ma-Dan, Gun-an-Noot's brother-in-law, had taken part in the brawl.

LeClair's death, however, was puzzling since he hadn't been at the Two Mile shindig. A Frenchman, and a rather quiet type, he had been a seaman but settled around Hazelton and ran a pack train. Apparently he met his death while on his way to pick up some straying horses.

With these details in his notebook, Kirby visited Gun-an-Noot's cabin.

The Indian was gone, but in the corral were four dead horses that Gun-an-Noot had apparently shot, maybe to deprive pursuers of their use. While checking the cabin Kirby noticed that all the ammunition was gone. Gun-an-Noot's wife, Sarah, was non-committal. Later, Kirby questioned Nah Gun, Gun-an-Noot's father, who said he didn't know a thing. Finally, late that same afternoon, Kirby got word that Peter Hi-ma-Dan had disappeared.

An inquest followed, with the jury of the opinion that the two white men were killed by Gun-an-Noot and his brother-in-law, Peter Hi-ma-Dan. Warrants were issued charging the pair with murder.

While it is a relatively simple matter to get a warrant, sometimes it is a lot more difficult to execute it. In the case of Gun-an-Noot it was thirteen years before any policeman put a hand on him — and then he surrendered voluntarily. While this performance may seem inept on the policemen's part, their task was as difficult as chasing fish in the sea.

Gun-an-Noot, wiry and agile, was the type whose moccasined feet took him through thickets with the ease and speed of a deer, and whose woodcraft was superlative. To him the whole Omineca country from Bell-Irving River to Klua-tan-tan was an open book. It is an area as big as France, and in it he knew every river and ridge, every slough and creek, every mountain trail.

First to pursue him were Constables Jim Kirby and Maitland-Dougall. Although they followed his trail for quite a while, they finally lost it. Then they found it again, pressed on for a week, then lost it once more. All that summer of 1906 relays of police and special constables, many of them expert bushmen and trackers, scoured the country. They checked every chance clue, but never came in sight of that will-o'-the-wisp, Gun-an-Noot.

Summer merged into fall, which in turn gave way to winter. Travel now was by snowshoe and dog team, and while the latter was a little quicker than hiking on foot, somehow it didn't bring the police any nearer to the outlaws. As one police party relieved another, old sourdoughs voiced their grudging admiration for the way the fugitives were holding out, and barroom wags occasionally transposed Simon's name from Gun-an-Noot to "Done-a-Scoot." But now even the police had some respect for a man who could be here, there, and everywhere; and finally nowhere at all. With this also came the realization that checking all the vague reports was a considerable drain on local police manpower.

The next spring headquarters at Victoria finally decided that local men had better stick to their day-to-day problems, while a special squad chased the outlaws. This group included Sergeant F.R. Murray, Constables Otway Wilkie and John Huggard, two guides and packers, plus two former members of the North-West Mounted Police. For good measure to these seven experienced men was added another well known northerner, Bert Glassey.

The plan called for two parties, one to go up the Stikine and come in over the Skeena watershed, checking the Yukon Telegraph Line cabins on the way. The other party, under Wilkie, would go in from Hazelton. In autumn, 1907, Wilkie left Hazelton for Takla Lake, 154 km (96 miles) away, where he established a base camp. From there he pushed to Bear Lake, reaching it on October 8. He and his party scoured part of the shoreline by raft, then went down the Bear and Sustut Rivers on an eight-day exploration, and returned in a blizzard. It was a sample of the cruel conditions faced by the searchers.

January found the party up on Kitkeah Pass "nearly out of provisions, but two prospectors, Bates and Olsen, had some goat meat." They searched the Otseka and Kettle Rivers and finally returned to Bear Lake without seeing a trace of Gun-an-Noot. Some fresh blazes on trees in the Otseka country roused their interest, but when they finally found the trail blazer he was a Fort Graham Indian.

On January 31, 1908, the frostbitten, bone-weary searchers started bucking the deep snow on the mountainous trail back to Hazelton. They struggled for ten days to cover the 154 km (96 miles).

The expedition could chalk up only one very slight gain. On the trail Wilkie arrested an Indian named Skookum House Tom, alias Sam Brown, "For theft of furs and refusing to obey a summons two years ago." Just to ensure that Sam stepped right along with him, Wilkie took possession of $500 worth of furs, plus $100 in cash. There was one other interesting note in Wilkie's report. An Indian at Bear Lake told him that one of their women had found a white man's head in perfect condition or "quite fresh" as the woman put it. The find was made near Teclapan River and remains another Northern mystery.

Wilkie's report had the final suggestion that it would be better to take up the chase in summer when horses could be employed. "Either that," he said, "or give up the chase until some reliable information is received."

Though some people at the time were inclined to smirk at what they thought the ineffectual nature of Wilkie's effort, his search party had travelled over 1,600 km (1,000 miles), mostly on foot and mostly under grueling winter conditions. How close they were to succeeding was revealed eleven years later when Peter Hi-ma-Dan gave his version. It turned out that the Wilkie party was unwittingly pushing the fugitives pretty hard. Peter revealed that at times they faced starvation but still had to keep moving to elude the police party. Sometimes they even trained their rifles on the group, almost tempted to end the chase by wounding or killing.

After Wilkie's departure no further organized searches were conducted for the fugitives. Season followed season, always the stray word coming by the grape vine that Simon had been seen somewhere or another. Once there was a report that Peter Hi-ma-Dan had left him, and, later still, word that Peter had drowned in a rapid.

In August 1914 outbreak of World War One dismissed from the public mind thoughts of Indian outlaws. Instead young men lined up at recruiting offices, and casualty lists were of greater interest than a search

The search for Gun-an-Noot continued in summer and winter. The photo at right shows the awesomely beautiful and rugged country in which he avoided capture for thirteen years.

for two Indians. Meantime, old-timers around Hazelton died, or left, and in the ceaseless departmental shuffling policemen moved in and out of Hazelton. New men were replaced by still newer men, who, but for an old reward notice, had never heard of Gun-an-Noot. The Indian was becoming a sort of legend — a far off memory.

Now and again, around campfires or in barrooms, Robin Hood type stories were told about him: he had slipped back to Kispiox in the dark of the moon, or had once been seen stalking the back alleys of Hazelton on some midnight visit. There was also a story that annually some Hazelton trader packed grub to a secret and distant rendezvous, then returned with Gun-an-Noot's furs. Lastly, there was the rumor that Gun-an-Noot had discovered a fabulously rich mine, and the more it was told the richer grew the ore.

A few people accidentally met Gun-an-Noot. One was Frank Chettleburgh who encountered Gun-an-Noot in March 1912. Frank, with his Kispiox guide, was locating some claims along the Pebble River in the

Ground Hog country, 240 km (150 miles) north of Hazelton. "I saw smoke across the valley one afternoon," he related, "so I asked my Indian who it might be."

"Just another Indian," was the somewhat evasive reply.

Chettleburgh wanted to meet the camper, but his Kispiox man was against it. "He doesn't like white men," was all he would say.

Frank, however, headed down the trail and made the lone camper's acquaintance. "He was an Indian, all right" he recalled. "Well set up, about thirty-five." He was also, despite the guide's warning, quite frank and friendly. He didn't give his name but asked who owned the cache by the river. Chettleburgh said he did. "I like one jam," said the Indian.

"Go ahead. Take what you want when you're down there," was Chettleburgh's friendly offer. A week later he found a chip of wood at the cache bearing the pencilled legend: "I take one jam."

Later, on a wet afternoon when he was making some notes, a shadow suddenly darkened Chettleburgh's tent flap. It was his chance-met Indian, bearing a hindquarter of caribou. "To pay for the jam," he said with simple dignity.

As Chettleburgh stood by his tent, watching the sturdy figure depart down the trail, his Kispiox guide remarked, "His name's Gun-an-Noot."

During World War One Mrs. Peter Hi-ma-Dan died at Kispiox. Before she breathed her last, however, she made a confession: she had killed Max LeClair. In her halting speech she told how in the early hours of the morning she was on her way to Two Mile to get Peter home from the party. On the way she met LeClair.

He'd had a drink or two and put his arms around her. She pushed him away, ran to her horse and yanked a rifle out of its scabbard. LeClair mounted and was making off when she fired to scare him. When she saw she had hit him, she started to cry. Then Gun-an-Noot, who had heard the shot, galloped up. He took her home, telling her to say nothing. He would take the blame for LeClair's death. But she must never reveal what happened on the trail that night.

Gun-an-Noot, center, with lawyer Stuart Henderson at left and George Biernes who suggested that the fugitive surrender.
On the opposite page Gun-an-Noot is shown with Constable Kelly, left, and Constable Cline who finally closed the case.

"When she and Gun-an-Noot got home," she said, "Nah Gun, his father, told them that McIntosh had also been shot and that Gun-an-Noot was sure to be blamed. He'd better go back in the mountains and stay there. It was on Nah Gun's advice," said the dying woman, "that Gun-an-Noot had taken to the hills."

The whole confession sounded unnatural. Why, if the man took off on his horse, did she have to shoot him? How could she shoot so accurately in the dark? How did Nah Gun know that McIntosh was dead? Later, from the Indian reserve, came another story. This time it was Peter Hi-ma-Dan who was drunk and shot LeClair, just as Peter's wife appeared on the scene. Thinking to protect her husband she had taken the blame in her death bed confession. Again there was a flaw — how could a drunk man plant a bullet in a man's back with such accuracy?

The confessions kept Gun-an-Noot's name very much alive in the Hazelton area, as did another police change that made Smithers the administrative headquarters of the district. Hazelton became a mere police post with one man in charge. His name was Cline. Though he became Sergeant Cline to a lot of latter day recruits in the old B.C. Provincial Police, and "Sperry" to his intimates, it was as "Dutch" Cline that Hazelton's pioneers knew him. His nickname originated because his bronze-tinted beard and hairy chest conjured up a likeness of a South African Dutchman.

One day in 1919 Sperry was watching some of the more important records being removed to the new Smithers office. Then, with a casual sweep of his hand, Cline removed the old Gun-an-Noot reward notice that had flaunted its fly-specked challenge to every office visitor for over ten years.

Those who knew Dutch Cline were aware that he never did anything without a purpose. His reason for removing the poster was to break the intimidating spell it held over the Indians who occasionally visited the office and to start a plan he was formulating. Now that he was boss of his one-man detachment, he decided to wind up the Gun-an-Noot case.

How he was going to do it is a story that pre-dates World War One when he and George Beirnes were partners running the mail by dog team from Hazelton to Kitimat on the frozen Skeena. Beirnes was still around, even had a little story to impart to his former partner. He'd met Gun-an-Noot away out in the Bear country. Although at first suspicious, Gun-an-Noot thawed somewhat when Beirnes gave him word of current fur prices. Seems that rumor was right, and Gun-an-Noot had a pal who was bringing out grub and taking away furs. But the pal was cheating him, lying about prices he was getting for fur. Gun-an-Noot felt friendly toward the white man who had wised him up, and in turn Beirnes suggested that he surrender. Gun-an-Noot looked thoughtful, then asked if it would be possible to have a lawyer.

"Sure," said Beirnes. "You tell us what day you'll come to Hazelton. We'll have a lawyer waiting to see you."

When Beirnes got back to Hazelton he and Cline arranged for Stuart Henderson, a famous Vancouver lawyer, to act as counsel. Henderson came to Hazelton, but on the day that Gun-an-Noot was to surrender his wife had a baby and he sent word that he had to stay with her.

Cline and Beirnes now had two problems: Henderson couldn't remain in Hazelton without arousing suspicion, and Gun-an-Noot was himself getting suspicious. Beirnes, it seems, had said something about collecting the reward and giving it to Gun-an-Noot to help defray legal costs. Gun-an-Noot was dubious about the plan. How could anyone collect a reward on him if he voluntarily gave himself up?

Simon Gun-an-Noot is buried beside his father in a grave which overlooks beautiful Bowser Lake.

Finally this doubt was smoothed out, and they set a new date for Gun-an-Noot to walk in. It was now Cline's turn to get the jitters. Supposing some old-timer with a long memory spotted Gun-an-Noot outside town, and tried to play the hero by bringing him in at gun point. In this event there could easily be another murder.

As things happened, however, Cline wasn't there for the surrender he had arranged. The day before he was subpoenaed to give evidence in a case at Prince Rupert. As he prepared to board the train, his relief, Constable John Kelly, stepped down to the platform.

They chatted for a minute, then Cline casually remarked, "You know, John, I wouldn't be surprised if Gun-an-Noot didn't give himself up one of these days."

Kelly, never a man for needless mirth, gave a wry smile and didn't answer. The whole thing was too ridiculous.

Next afternoon as he stood behind the office counter making some entries in a book, a shadow-like, mocassin-clad figure suddenly stood before him. "Yes," said Kelly, looking up.

"I'm Gun-an-Noot," said the impassive stranger. "I've come to give myself up."

Before Kelly could decide whether it was a gag, Stuart Henderson and Beirnes were alongside the Indian.

The trial was held in Vancouver that fall. Inspector Tom Parsons of Prince George took the famous fugitive to Vancouver. When he was brought from his cell, Gun-an-Noot, blinking shyly, stuck out his wrists for handcuffs. With a smile Parsons said, "No handcuffs."

As Stuart Henderson had anticipated, the hearing was brief. In fact so outdated was the crime that the few people in court gave more glances to the clock than to the impassive Indian sitting in the prisoner's box. The crown had no evidence to produce, and the verdict was not guilty. On October 8, 1918, Simon Gun-an-Noot stepped into the street, no longer a wanted man.

Months later his brother-in-law, Peter Hi-ma-Dan, took his turn in the dock. "There was not a tittle of evidence produced to connect him with either murder, and he was discharged at the preliminary hearing," Sutherland recalled.

Gun-an-Noot went back to the Skeena watershed, to the country he knew and loved. It was there he was trapping, just north of Bowser Lake, when illness overtook him in 1933. He died that October. Some of his fellow tribesmen packed his body nine miles to bury him beside his father on Bowser Lake. People remembered that Simon once packed his father's body forty miles to do the same thing.

It was four months before Indian trapper Tom Campbell brought word to the outside world that Gun-an-Noot had died. The news brought a momentary clatter to telegraph sounders from Prince Rupert to Jasper, and in every one of the lonely little cabins along the 1,500-mile long Yukon Telegraph Line from Quesnel to Dawson City. Then the event was largely forgotten, except in B.C.'s vast northwest. Even today when old-timers meet around campfires and in living rooms in the Hazelton, Omineca and Babine country, legendary Gun-an-Noot lives on.

Constable M. Graburn: First Mountie to be Murdered

On a snowy November evening in 1879 in the
Cypress Hills of what is today Alberta-Saskatchewan,
Constable M. Graburn was shot in the back. Who
murdered him or why remains a mystery.

Star Child, who was tried for Graburn's murder but acquitted.

Constable Graburn's grave site is today part of Alberta's Cypress Hills Provincial Park. Saskatchewan also has a park in the picturesque Cypress Hills, while the Federal Government has declared the area around Fort Walsh a National Historic Park.

In the 130-km (80-mile) wide Cypress Hills which straddle the Saskatchewan-Alberta border at the U.S. boundary is a lonely grave and a cairn with the inscription:

MURDER OF CONSTABLE GRABURN

Constable Marmaduke Graburn, NWMP, was shot and killed by unknown persons in the Cypress Hills November 17, 1879.

He was the first Mounted Police killed by violence since the force was formed in 1873.

Star Child, a Blood Indian, was accused of the murder but was acquitted in 1881.

Although Graburn was the first officer murdered on duty, his fellow officers had been expecting such an incident. Indeed, they were surprised that the force had been in existence for five years before a policeman died other than by sickness or accident.

As John Peter Turner noted in *The North-West Mounted Police,* the official two-volume history of the force: "It was a remarkable fact, often commented upon in barrack rooms and at lonely campfires, that during five years of strenuous work upon the plains, dealing with all manner of people, many of them eminently worthy of the titles 'desperado' and

Map courtesy Saskatchewan Museum of Natural History.

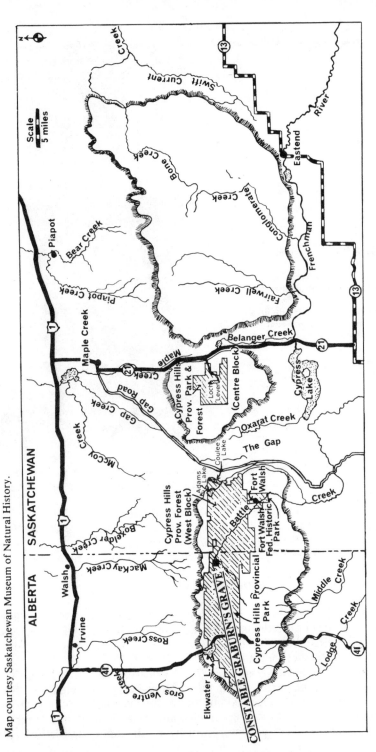

The Cypress Hills of Alberta-Saskatchewan

'gunman', not a single member of the force had lost his life by human violence. Nor had any member of the force pressed a trigger against his fellow man. And yet there had been no halfway measures, no faltering, no tendency to sidestep difficult and dangerous situations, nothing but a fixed and resolute determination to establish law and order throughout a hitherto unbridled realm of some 250,000 square miles — a striking contrast to the conditions existing in the country immediately south of the international boundary, where one of the first axioms of life had for long been 'kill or be killed'.''

Examples of the ''no tendency to sidestep difficult and dangerous situations'' were many in the Cypress Hills in the late 1870s. This was the period when thousands of Sioux, Assiniboine and other Indians from the U.S. sought refuge in Canada after the 1876 massacre of Lieutenant-Colonel George A. Custer and the 231 men who rode with him, including his two brothers and brother-in-law. Time after time a few Mounties rode into Indian encampments to arrest troublemakers amid masses of angry warriors. Many of these warriors were armed with rifles and belts of ammunition taken from Custer's 7th Cavalry troopers and wore cavalrymen's scalps on their belts. One of them, Sitting Bull's nephew, boasted that he had killed twenty-three of Custer's men with his ''coup stick'' — a weapon resembling a baseball bat except that a round stone was encased in rawhide at one end.

A typical instance of the policeman's attitude of ''no faltering'' is related by John Peter Turner in his official history of the NWMP. It occurred in May 1877 and involved Superintendent James M. Walsh, commander of the Fort Walsh police post established in the Cypress Hills two years before. Walsh learned that Sitting Bull, famous chief of the Sioux, would join the thousands of his tribesmen who had sought refuge in the Cypress Hills. He decided to meet Sitting Bull and set out with a sergeant, three constables and two scouts — Louis Leveille and Gabriel Soloman. After two days riding they reached their destination, passing a grave which they later learned contained a warrior who had died after being badly wounded in the Custer massacre.

Walsh impressed on Sitting Bull the necessity for obeying the law. The consequence of not doing so was that the Sioux would be sent back across the border — although Walsh did not explain how fewer than 100 red coats at Fort Walsh would evict thousands of seasoned Indian warriors.

As John Turner wrote in Volume One of *The North-West Mounted Police:* ''That night Walsh and his men slept in the Sioux camp. While they were preparing to leave next morning an episode occurred which gave the Sioux a profound reminder of how fearlessly the law which they had promised to respect would be enforced.

''Three Indian riders trailing five extra horses came in from the south. The men were recognized by one of Walsh's scouts as South Assiniboines from the Missouri. One of them, White Dog, a notorious warrior, had been offered 100 horses by Sitting Bull the previous year to join the Sioux in the campaign that summer against the Americans. Scout Gabriel Solomon identified three of the five horses as the property of Father De

Superintendent James M. Walsh
and Chief Sitting Bull.
The background photo shows
the Cypress Hills in 1883.

Corby, a Roman Catholic priest who had lately been in the Cypress Hills. Walsh was at once told about it, and Leveille was instructed to inspect the horses closely with Solomon, lest the accusation turn out to be a mistake. Leveille agreed with Solomon that the horses were stolen, and the superintendent decided to make an example of the thieves. Instructions were given to Sergeant McCutcheon to make the arrest.

"By this time White Dog and his companions had mixed in with a group of 50 or 60 Sioux warriors, engrossed in telling of their trip across the plains. Accompanied by two constables, McCutcheon strolled over to the Indian group and through the interpreter apprised White Dog of his intentions. The latter demanded the reason, and upon being told of the charge against him, indignantly retorted that the horses were his, that he would not give them up, much less submit to arrest. Sensing the possibility of an argument in which McCutcheon might be hard put to hold his ground, Walsh stepped forward with the remaining constable and joined the group. At once there was excitement; the news spread through the camp. White Dog was doubtlessly confident that the Sioux would support him. In the face of the insignificant party of white men confronting him he became boastful and defiant.

"Calling the interpreter to his side, Walsh made small account of the Indian's haughty refusal to submit: 'White Dog, you say you will neither be arrested nor surrender these horses?' Then placing a hand on the Indian's shoulder: 'I arrest you for theft.'

"A bomb had fallen on the camp.

"Scouts had caught the horses and brought them to the rear. McCutcheon was ordered to disarm the three Indians, and before any of those present could realize what was taking place, the Assiniboines were in custody. All who saw it were electrified by the stark courage and suddenness with which Walsh had acted; even more so, when the superintendent ordered one of his men to bring forward a pair of leg-irons.

"Holding these before the amazed White Dog, he said: 'White Dog, tell me where you got those horses, how you got them and what you intend doing with them, or I shall put these irons upon you and take you to Fort Walsh.'

"All were silent, and seeing no possibility of assistance from the Sioux who were now crowding around in hundreds, the Assiniboine stated that when passing over the plains east of the Cypress Hills he had seen some horses wandering unattended and had taken them; he had not known it was wrong to do so, as it was customary in the Milk River country south of the line to seize horses found in that way, and return them to their owner only if called for.

"Though the superintendent suspected him of lying, his words were accepted; but White Dog was warned against molesting any property, no matter how or where found, north of the line.

"Defiance showed in White Dog's piercing eyes. He felt his position keenly — he had been disgraced in the presence of the onlooking Sioux, who had already learned a lesson long to be remembered. Then unable to suppress his feelings, the crestfallen Assiniboine glared at Walsh and said: 'I shall meet you again.'

"Walsh caught his words through the interpreter, and as the Indian turned to go with his companions, he was ordered to halt and repeat what he had said, being reminded that there should be no misunderstanding. He refused to do so.

" 'Withdraw those words you just uttered,' the superintendent shouted as he held the leg-irons before the silent and solemn Indian. 'If you do not, I shall take you to Fort Walsh.'

"The Indian replied that he had not meant to make a threat, and though it was apparent that he was again lying, the three horse thieves were dismissed. Later the horses were delivered to their rightful owner."

While the bravery of Walsh and his few men had won the respect of the Sioux, a potentially far more dangerous confrontation was brewing. Walsh had barely returned to Fort Walsh when a Saulteau Indian Chief, Little Child, rode in and requested help. The chief and the rest of his band were camped about 48 km (30 miles) to the northeast and were worried about the invasion of the tribes from the U.S.

Fort Walsh in 1876. The fort has been rebuilt and today is part of popular Fort Walsh National Historic Park.

As John Turner wrote: "Little Child was a remarkably fine type of Indian, completely belying his name, as he was all of six feet, stalwart, handsome, lithe as a cat, intelligent and broad-minded. He was a frequent visitor at the fort and had often been assured that the Mounted Police were in control of the country, that their purpose was to guarantee the safety of all, and that every person was to have the right to his just possessions. Indians were to cease making war; the white man was their friend.

"The perturbed chief related that about 250 lodges of South Assiniboines had arrived from the region of the Bear Paw Mountains in Montana and had made camp about half a mile from that of the Saulteaux. The newcomers had set themselves up as a law unto themselves and had given notice that they would monopolize the buffalo hunting, saying they had little respect for the white man's authority. Though they were United States agency Indians, with no rights on Canadian soil, they had ordered the smaller camp to join them and bow to Assiniboine hunting

rules. One of the chiefs of the Assiniboines, Crow's Dance, had stated that he would gather in all smaller encampments and would take over exclusive power in the Cypress Hills country. Little Child had refused to comply, and shortly afterwards the would-be Assiniboine dictator had turned up with several hundred warriors in full war regalia to enforce his demands. Little Child had no more than 30 fighting men, but courageously enough, in spurning the other's orders had stated: 'I am a British Indian on British soil, and I will not submit. The only chief I will obey is the White Chief at Fort Walsh.'

"In reply Crow's Dance had boasted: 'When your red-coated friends come to my camp you will be there to see how I use them.'

"Then he and his followers had attacked the Saulteau camp, tearing down lodges, shooting dogs and threatening the lives of the women and children. The Saulteaux had offered no resistance and had fled for safety to the shelter of some wooded hills to the north.

"Little Child brought word to Superintendent Walsh that Crow's Dance had announced he would cut out the heart of the 'Chemoganish' (Redcoat) and eat it, if the latter dared to come to his camp.

" 'We'll see about that later,' the superintendent remarked.

"In no more than an hour, Walsh, Surgeon Kittson, Sub-Inspr. Edwin Allen, 14 men and Louis Leveille, the guide, were in the saddle headed for the Assiniboine camp. Failure to support Little Child in his plea for help would only invite ridicule and worse. Walsh knew that one breach of faith would create a crisis in Indian circles unpleasant to contemplate. In a case like this there could be no choice and no wavering. The surgeon had been ordered to accompany the patrol as there was likely to be bloodshed, and as the little group left the valley and rode across the prairie, there were doubtless many conflicting but silent emotions.

"Late that night (May 25) the police, with Little Child guiding them, arrived at the site of the alleged violence. Here a halt was made while the ground was reconnoitered. Scout Leveille expressed the opinion that the Assiniboine camp had apparently moved northward, and without stopping to rest, Walsh and his men cautiously followed the trail. After riding for another hour, they made a second halt. Horses were unsaddled and turned out to graze under strong picket. The men rested until about two o'clock. While moving slowly forward just as dawn was breaking, Leveille and Little Child sighted the Assiniboine camp. A third halt was made and all had breakfast. Arms were inspected; the men were told that they were about to face several hundred hostile warriors. Exteme danger lay ahead; the leaders were to be arrested. Orders were to be strictly obeyed.

"Walsh and Leveille ascended a nearby hill to survey the camp. Everything was silent, and Walsh decided to attempt a surprise arrest, despite the fact that the patrol was overwhelmingly outnumbered. A small butte near a little lake was selected as the point to which the police would retire with the captives. Surgeon Kittson with three men were stationed there and instructed to build a breastwork of stones in case a fight ensued. If necessary a man was to ride to Fort Walsh at all speed for assistance, but Kittson was to hold his ground as a rallying point.

"At a lively trot Walsh headed his men toward the inner lodges of the camp. A few moments would decide the issue. Quickly locating the lodge of Crow's Dance and surrounding it, the superintendent sprang from his horse and entered. No words were wasted in overture or argument. With a few curt invectives, for which he was noted, the superintendent reappeared almost immediately with the startled Assiniboine chief in tow.

"A thunderbolt had fallen. Without ceremony Crow's Dance, another chief named Crooked Arm, and 18 of their henchmen were pressed into a group by themselves and bustled off. Two other leaders, Bear's Down and Blackfoot, were then rounded up. By this time pandemonium had swept the sleeping camp. No weapons had been drawn; no shots heralded a bloody conflict. Silent courage, taut with the might of right, had won a swift and signal victory. The captives were taken to 'Kittson's Butte', and a second breakfast was eaten while word was being sent to the Assiniboines that they would be spoken to shortly.

"Eventually Walsh lectured the remaining leaders of the Assiniboines and warned them against a repetition. He told them he would take the captives to Fort Walsh for trial, that the head chief and 12 others would be retained for that purpose.

"More than a day was expended in carrying out the little sortie, and the trial took place the day after the return. Eleven of the younger Indians were discharged by Walsh with a severe caution as to their future conduct. The following day Assistant Commissioner Irvine, who arrived from the West, adjudged the cases of Crow's Dance and Crooked Arm. The chief received six months' imprisonment at hard labour, and the other, two months. News of the occurrence spread far and wide . . . instilling a deep respect for the North-West Mounted Police."

The Blood Indians, however, were not impressed, even though they were Canadian. They were camped about 16 km (10 miles) northwest of Fort Walsh around what was known as the "Horse Camp." This camp was one of several established by the NWMP for horses that needed a rest or were suffering from ailments. For reasons unknown the Bloods were particularly hostile to this camp. One theory is that it was perhaps in an area which was a favorite with the Bloods or beside a trail the Bloods used as an escape route after horse stealing sorties to ranches or other Indian camps.

Whatever the reason, the Bloods were a constant nuisance, appearing every day to beg for food or anything else they could get. One, Star Child, was particularly persistent and seemed content to live solely by begging.

In November 1879 among those at Horse Camp were scout Jules Quesnelle, and Constables Marmaduke Graburn and George Johnston, both of whom had enlisted in Ottawa and travelled West together. On November 17, Johnston stayed in camp to cook while Graburn and Quesnelle went out with the horses. While the work was easy the hours were long — from 5 a.m. to about 5.30 p.m. On the way back from the pasture the two stopped at a garden plot where the men had planted vegetables. When they reached Horse Camp Graburn discovered that he had left his lariat and axe at the garden and returned to get them.

With nightfall snow began falling and as time passed the men at

Horse Camp became increasingly concerned at Graburn's absence. Finally they went looking for him but because of the blackness soon gave up. Next morning they sent word to Fort Walsh where Superintendent Crozier immediately dispatched a search party, among whom were Constable R. McCutcheon and guides Jerry Potts and Louis Leveille.

The search party soon found the tracks of Graburn's horse, leading off in a southerly direction, and was surprised to find that two other sets of hoof prints joined those of Graburn's pony a short way down the trail. The trackers had no difficulty following the trail, but could not be sure if the three riders had travelled together, or if the two unknown riders had simply been following the young constable. They were quite sure, however, that since the two unknown riders were riding unshod ponies, they were probably Indians.

Still farther down the trail was a place where it looked as though Graburn's horse had lunged forward and nearby was a large pool of blood. Farther along was another massive blood stain that the trackers would have overlooked had not one of the horses kicked up the snow covering it. The searchers concentrated on this area and nearby at the bottom of a brush-filled coulee Constable McCutcheon found Graburn's body. He had been shot in the back.

The following day, November 19, scout Jerry Potts led a search party in an attempt to track down the killers. They found Constable Graburn's horse tied to a tree in dense timber, shot twice in the head. At that point the search had to be abandoned because a chinook obliterated the trail.

An 1879 photo of the NWMP horse camp where Constable Graburn was murdered.

In his official report Commissioner Macleod noted: "There is no doubt but the foul deed was perpetrated by two Indians, but we have not been able to fix the guilt upon the murderers. I feel sure they will be discovered, as when they are across the line and think themselves safe, they will be certain to say something about it which will lead to their detection, and other Indians will be sure to let us know. I am confident there was nothing in the act itself to lead to the belief that the Indians had changed in their feelings towards us, and that when the facts come out they will show that the atrocious crime was committed in revenge for some real or fancied injury done to the murderer or one of his family, not necessarily by a policeman but by some white man. All his comrades mourned the sad fate of poor young Graburn deeply, as he was a great favourite among us all."

Although a thorough search had been carried out, there was no trace of the prime suspect, Star Child, one of those who had harassed Graburn and the others at Horse Camp. The following summer, however, two Blood braves were picked up for horse stealing and imprisoned at Fort Walsh.

After long interrogation the guards learned that the two braves had been camped near Horse Camp at the time of the murder. Major Crozier at Fort Walsh suspected the two Bloods knew more of the murder than they were telling and decided to hold them, hoping to get further information from them. The two braves, suspecting they were being held for more than horse stealing, tried to escape. They were abetted by their wives, who passed rifles to them as they ran from the stockade.

Inspector Sam Steele, who was also at Fort Walsh at the time, later wrote: "Crozier, Cotton and Kennedy were playing tennis in front of the fort and, when they saw the escape, followed the fugitives. I sent the first men who turned out after them, mounted. They caught the Indians in about half a mile. Ignoring their levelled rifles, they rode at them and soon had them back in their old quarters in the guard-room. Their attempt to escape having failed, the two asked to see Crozier in his quarters at midnight, and after the windows had been covered with blankets so that no light could be seen from the outside, they gave him the name, description and full particulars of the Indian who had murdered Grayburn . . . ."

Major Crozier sent a message to Commissioner James Macleod who was in Fort Benton on business that Star Child was hiding in the Bear Paw Mountains. Commissioner Macleod tried to persuade the U.S. authorities to apprehend and return the fugitive, but the Fort Benton sheriff wanted $5,000 for his trouble. Since Macleod had no such sum at his disposal, Star Child remained free for a while longer. The NWMP bided their time until the fugitive returned to Canada.

Wrote Steele: "This did not present itself until 1881, when Sergeant Patterson at Macleod learned that he (Star Child) was in the Blood camp (about 25 miles south of Fort Macleod) and proceeded there, accompanied by Jerry Potts and two constables. They arrived at dawn and went to the lodge in which the murderer, Star Child by name, was concealed, their intention being to take him without arousing the camp, which, it was believed was hostile. The Indian came out at dawn, fully armed; covering

Restored Fort Walsh, with the lower photo showing a NWMP barracks. Up to fifty men shared a barrack room, their bunks made first from wooden poles, then later from boards and trestles. Mattresses were gunny sacks stuffed with hay, while bedding was two blankets and a buffalo robe. Men and horses worked hard. In 1880, for instance, Constable Armour and his team travelled from April to November over 4,800 km (3,000 miles).

Patterson with his rifle, he told him that he would shoot if he moved a hand or foot; but the sergeant as a ruse, spoke as if addressing someone behind Star Child, causing him to turn his head, whereupon Patterson threw himself upon him. In the struggle the gun went off, rousing the whole camp . . . . . In the meantime Patterson had the murderer underneath him while Jerry Potts, Strangling Wolf, One Spot and Constable Wilson . . . kept the remainder at bay. The sergeant then took Star Child towards Macleod at the full speed of his horse . . . followed by the majority of the band as far as the fort, where they were forced to halt and turn back . . . ."

Star Child was charged with murder and locked up at Fort Macleod. According to Sam Steele, he confessed to the murder, although if he gave a reason it has never been revealed. Despite the confession and corroborating evidence, at his trial in Macleod on May 18, 1881, the six-man all-white jury voted for acquittal. There are suggestions that the jury feared Blood reprisals if they found Star Child guilty. Anyway, there was nothing Colonel Macleod, acting as stipendary magistrate, could do but turn the accused man loose.

An argument against the supposition that the jury "ran scared," however, is that several former policemen were among its six members. Also they deliberated nearly twenty-four hours before returning a verdict. RCMP historian S.W. Horrall wrote of the decision: "As one of the jurors pointed out later . . . the crown's case rested entirely upon Starchild's own boastful statement that he had killed Graburn. There was no corroborating evidence. Moreover it was not unusual for young Indians (Starchild was about 19 years old at the time of Graburn's murder) to boast of deeds they had not actually committed in order to gain recognition. Most historians of the NWMP, however, have assumed that Starchild was the murderer. The truth of the matter will never be known."

If Star Child were guilty, he did not escape punishment altogether. Two years later, he ran a herd of stolen horses into Canada from the U.S. and was arrested by Sergeant Ashe. On July 5, 1883, he was sentenced to four years in Stony Mountain Penitentiary.

Afterwards he returned to the Blood Reservation and was later hired by Superintendent R.B. Deane as a police scout. In 1888 two whiskey traders were arrested because of his work for the force. "Out of several Indian scouts that I have tried none have proved to be worth their salt but Starchild," Deane noted in a report. "He did some good work for us and I did not expect to replace him."

In 1889, however, Star Child carried on a love affair with the Indian wife of a white man and was discharged from the force. He died a short time later of tuberculosis.

As for the murdered Graburn, his grave rests on a bench overlooking the creek which was named after him. While the plaque on his cairn gives about all the information known of the murder, it does not mention a tragic sequel. On May 23, 1882, Constable George Johnston, Graburn's friend who had enlisted with him, was accidentally shot and killed by another member of the force. He lies buried at Fort Walsh, about a mile from Graburn's grave.

Today's memorial to
Constable M. Graburn. The
inscription reads:
"In memory of Marmaduke
Graburn, died 17 November 1879.
This monument was erected by
his comrades of B & F Divisions
of the N.W.M.P. as a token
of the esteem in which
they held him."

A selection of HERITAGE HOUSE titles

B.C. Provincial Police Stories

Volume 1 contains stories of true cases, reconstructed from police files and B.C. provincial archives by Deputy Commissioner **Cecil Clark**. Read about the man who was hanged by a thread, tragedy stalked the Silver Trail, the men who were murdered by mistake, and fifteen others.

Volume 2 includes tales of murder on Okanagan Lake, West Kootenay's tragic miner who died eight times, when Death rode a pinto pony, the cremation of Siboo Singh, Kitwancool drums that throbbed a war dance, the parking ticket that killed three men, and the hangman's tree at Lillooet.

The rowboat policemen, the murdering McLeans, Sperry Cline—one of a kind, tracking an insane killer, canine policemen, Peace River posting, and Skook Davidson—Northern Legend are some of the twenty-plus yarns featuring Cecil Clark's popular style in Volume 3.

Vol. 1 • ISBN 1-895811-77-5 • 128 pages • $9.95

Vol. 2 • ISBN 1-895811-83-X • 128 pages • $9.95

Vol. 3 • ISBN 1-895811-75-9 • 160 pages • $12.95

Kootenai Brown
Canada's Unkown Frontiersman

William Rodney tells about Brown's adventurous life in Canada, which began in 1862 during the Cariboo gold rush. He later became a B.C. policeman, Pony Express rider, buffalo hunter, and head scout for the Rocky Mountain Rangers during the 1885 Riel Rebellion. He helped to establish Waterton Lakes National Park.

ISBN 1-895811-31-7 • 256 pages • $17.95

West Kootenay
The Pioneer Years

Nine chapters include Rossland, the golden city; Ainsworth, West Kootenay's first town; Nelson and the fabled Silver King Mine; and ghost towns of the silvery Slocan. Another of **Garnet Basque**'s books—well illustrated in colour and indexed.

ISBN 1-895811-42-2 • 168 pages • $17.95

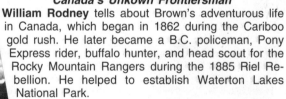

Carving the Western Path

These companion volumes offer anecdotal accounts of B.C.'s pioneer roadbuilders, railway barons, and sternwheel captains. **Bob Harvey** assesses the impact of CPR's growth strategies on the evolution of B.C.'s transportation. He writes of the difficulties early roadbuilders had claiming a share of the high passes and recalls how sternwheelers dominated the rivers and lakes of B.C.

By River, Rail and Road Through B.C.'s Southern Mountains
ISBN 1-895811-62-7 • 240 pages • $18.95

By River, Rail, and Road Through Central and Northern B.C.
ISBN 1-89811-74-0 • 240 pages • $18.95

The Death of Albert Johnson
Mad Trapper of Rat River

It took a posse of trappers, soldiers, Indians, and the RCMP six weeks and four shoot-outs amid blizzards and numbing cold to bring their quarry to bay. Who was Albert Johnson, the murderer and subject of one of the great manhunts of all time? This book tells the story.

ISBN 0-919214-16-9 • 96 pages • $8.95

Outlaws & Lawmen of Western Canada

If you enjoyed Volume 1, there's more drama in Volume 2. Read of Jess Williams—the first man hanged in Calgary, Almighty Voice's murder of a policeman in 1895 that caused six other deaths, B.C.'s hanging that set a world record, the McLean Gang, Manitoba's first official outlaw, and many others. 80 photos and maps.

Volume 3 includes the Mad Trapper of Rat River, Saskatchewan's midnight massacre, Yukon's Christmas Day assassins, blazing guns at Banff, B.C.'s murdering cannibal, stone-age murderers, Winnipeg's Prairie Strangler and others. 100 photos and maps.

Vol. 2 • ISBN 1-895811-85-6 • 128 pages • $10.95
Vol. 3 • ISBN 0-919214-88-6 • 160 pages • $11.95